COMES THIS MORNING

WITHDRAWN

# NORMA DeSHIELDS BROWN

# Joy

## COMES THIS MORNING

JOY COMES THIS MORNING

A New Spirit Novel

ISBN-13: 978-0-373-83035-0
ISBN-10:　　0-373-83035-1

This publication contains the opinions and ideas of its author.
It is intended to provide helpful and informative material on the
subject matter covered. It is sold with the understanding that the
publisher is not engaged in rendering psychological, medical, or other
professional services. If expert assistance or counseling is needed, the
services of a competent professional should be sought.

www.kimanipress.com

**Printed in U.S.A.**

I dedicate this book to my only child,
Brian Christopher DeShields.

Thank you Brian, for teaching me how to love
and give unconditionally.

My life has been so very blessed by you.

Your fun loving spirit will always be with me and I look
forward to the day we will see each other again.

Give Jesus a big hug and kiss for me.

Mommy

## SPECIAL THANKS

To Jesus, my Lord, best friend, counselor, teacher, father, peace, joy, provider, healer, comforter...my everything. Thank you for saving me, keeping me and using me for your kingdom.

To my awesome, wonderful and extremely handsome husband, Jeffery—I cannot thank you enough for choosing me to be your helpmate. You are everything that I prayed for and more. I love you beyond words and I look forward to spending my life with you.

To Reverend James T. Meeks, my spiritual father. Thank you for supporting me and helping me with this project. Thank you for being obedient to the call of God on your life, which has blessed me beyond words.

To Glenda Howard and the great staff of Harlequin/ Kimani Press, I just want to say a big thank-you for taking this project and allowing me to share it with the world. You guys have been wonderful, and I look forward to a long and rewarding partnership with you and many more books to come.

To my wonderful mother, Irene, who didn't listen to the doctors when they said you would never have children. Thank you for all your love, support and prayers.

To my sister and best friend Monique—I love you, girl. Thank you for always encouraging me and letting me borrow my nephew Brandon, who has been a second son to me. Thanks for always being there for me and listening when I need to talk.

To my nephew Brandon, who is unlike any young man I know. Your love for Christ is truly inspiring. Thank you for being there for me and sharing your life with your "aintee." I love you, and I can't wait to see what God does in your life.

To my sister Manon, I thank God for bringing you into my life. I know God has a good and perfect plan for you as you journey through your life and purpose.

To my daughters, Jailyn and Jada, I just want you to know that God truly blessed me with two wonderful children when you came into my life. I am very blessed to be able to impart some of me into your life. I look forward to watching you grow into beautiful, strong women of God.

To my new family—mother-in-law, Annie, father-in-law, Richard, Shelly, Shoinna, Reggie and all my nieces and nephews, I just want to thank you for welcoming me into the Brown clan. I love all of you.

To my girlfriends Wanda, Wendy, Cheryl, Pat, Cathy and Jerine—thank you for being there in good times and bad. Without you, life's journey would be very lonely and boring. Thanks for letting me cry on your shoulders, call you anytime—day or night—and for praying with and for me.

To the memory of my good friend Chemin Abner, who taught me how to be free and to love being me, and who showed me qualities in myself I didn't even know I had.

To the memory of my loving father, Norman, who made me feel so special and loved and allowed me to be "daddy's little girl." Thanks for taking such good care of me, and thanks for taking care of Brian in Heaven. Keep the light on for me.

Norma

# FOREWORD

In a time like this, tragedy fills the news reports daily. There are countless reports of violent acts committed in our own country as well as all over the world. Many people have lost hope, many have lost the desire to live and many have lost a desire to love. Jesus knew that we would need guidelines in this life. He knew we would encounter sadness, hopelessness and despair. He knew that we were not going to make it on our own. He also knew how to help us. You know the Scriptures; the disciples had an opportunity to be alone with the Teacher. They could have asked Jesus to teach them how to raise the dead. They could have asked Jesus to teach them how to cure the sick, yet they asked Jesus to teach them how to pray. Jesus knew that the answer to that question would also prepare the disciples for what was ahead. Not only the disciples; Jesus knew that His answer would also prepare us.

We are not going to make it, be happy and filled with the joy of the Lord unless we pray. Prayer is an awareness of the power of God. Prayer acknowledges that this is God's world and nothing catches Him by surprise. Prayer is an attitude that says, there is nothing He can't handle, and all things are possible to them that believe. To develop a daily prayer life you will need discipline. This devotional can easily become an impetus to prayer. We thank God for Norma DeShields Brown, who has demonstrated that through prayer God can restore your joy. Norma has provided us with a guideline that easily allows us to nurture our prayer lives. Each day starts off with a scripture and a word of encouragement. Meditate on the scripture in the morning, talk with your Father and tell Him what's on your mind. My prayer is that God will speak directly to you as you speak to Him.

"But his delight is in the law of the Lord; and in his law doth he meditate both day and night." *Psalms* 1:2

Pastor James T. Meeks

Dear Friend,

I am so glad to be able to share with you some encouragement to start your day. God has been so good to me that I just can't keep it all to myself!

This devotional came about through journal writing after my only child, Brian, was murdered in 1994. At that time in my life, I was a fairly new Christian, just beginning to develop a personal relationship with the Lord. Even though I was confused as to why this happened to me, I had a strange peace that surpassed my understanding. God's unlimited grace enabled me to endure the impossible, allowing me day-to-day to move forward and grow in the process. I also knew that my son was alive with God through salvation in the Lord Jesus Christ. Therefore, we would see each other again and be together for all eternity.

God put on my heart to begin to write my thoughts and feelings down and to share my growth with others. I am not a professional writer. I don't have a long list of letters behind my name. I am just an everyday woman who has given her life to Christ and has allowed Him to heal me, deliver me and use me. God will do the same for you, if you let Him.

I believe that each page of this book was anointed by God and given to me from the Holy Spirit. I know you will be blessed, even as I was in writing it.

It is my hope that you will be inspired, encouraged and enlightened as you walk in and out of your journey of life with God. Although the journey is not always easy, you will make it. I can say that with confidence, because I did. Be blessed.

Yours in Christ,

Norma DeShields Brown

# CONTENTS

# New Beginnings

# THIS DAY BELONGS TO THE LORD

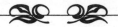

*This is the day which the Lord hath made; we will rejoice and be glad in it.*

—Psalms 118:24

Do you realize that today is a day that has never been seen before by any man? God has blessed you and allowed you to share this day on earth. He woke you up this morning and gave you new mercy (Lamentations 3:22, 23). That is worth rejoicing about, don't you think? Give God the glory for your life today!

What are your plans for this year? What has God put into your spirit to do? Have you given it much thought? If not, today would be a good day to sit down and write out your dreams and goals. It has been said that people who actually have their goals written down on paper are the most successful in achieving their goals.

If your life is not where you want to be, it's up to you to change it. Don't get frustrated and mad, make a plan. Get started now! Procrastination is a dream killer. Make a commitment and stick to the plan. Just do it! Make God the CEO of your life and put your plan before Him. He will direct your paths.

There is a worship song that we sometimes sing in our church entitled, "This Is The Day." The song's lyrics remind us that no matter what is going on in our life, we are blessed because we have God and therefore we should always be thankful.

This is a blessed day. It's a blessed year! Rise up and rejoice, for your blessings are on the way!

# YOUR DESIRES CAN HAPPEN

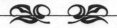

*Delight yourself also in the Lord, and He shall give you the desires of your heart.*

—Psalms 37:4

*W*hat a great promise of God! God will give us the desires of our hearts if we delight in Him. Wouldn't life be wonderful if we had all our desires fulfilled? We would be on cloud nine every day. God wants to do just that, but He has one requirement for us — that we delight also in the Lord. What exactly does that mean? The word *delight* means to be soft or pliable; to desire. God wants us to be soft and pliable in His hands and to desire Him above all things. When we have this kind of intimate relationship with God, He can pour out the blessings of our desires upon us because we will only desire those things that bring Him glory.

I want to be soft and pliable in God's hands. Even as I am being molded and made into the image of Christ, I know that God is well pleased with me. He loves me just as I am, and my desire is to become more like Him. Do you want these things, too?

Join me today in asking God to change you into the godly person He created you to be. The Lord loves you. Give Him your heart today. Allow Him to mold you and direct you. Seek Him first, and He will reveal to you the things that are good for you. Give Him full reign in your life. Spend as much time as you can building an intimate relationship with Him, learning of Him and receiving from Him. I guarantee you will fall in love with God, too, just as I have and you will soon delight in the Lord and He will give you the desires of your heart!

# GIVE US THIS DAY

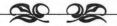

*What shall I render unto the Lord for all his benefits toward me?*
—Psalms 116:12

Today God has a load of benefits and blessings just for you! For starters, He woke you up this morning. Now, the rest of the day can be a breeze—if we choose for it to be.

God does His part by giving us life. We have free will and must choose how we are going to live the life He has given us. God has already provided everything we need. He knows what is going to happen long before we know. The provision is there. The question that we must ask ourselves is—are we going to take it? God's job is to provide, our job is to receive.

When God led the children of Israel out of Egypt into the wilderness, He fed them manna from Heaven each day. "And they gathered it every morning, every man according to his eating; and when the sun waxed hot it melted" (Exodus 16:21). He cared for them day by day and not in advance. I believe this was to teach them to trust God each day for their provision. He wanted to show them that He would supply all their needs and that they could trust Him to provide their daily bread.

Enjoy your day today. Receive the benefits God has provided for you. If you do not know what God has provided for you, read the Bible and find out. The promises are real and available to everyone who believes. When you know what God has for you, it will not be so easy for the enemy to upset you. Choose life!

# BE SET FREE

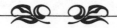

*The Spirit of the Lord is upon me, because He hath anointed me to preach the gospel to the poor; He hath sent me to heal the brokenhearted, to preach deliverance to the captives, and recovering of sight to the blind, to set at liberty them that are bruised.*

—Luke 4:18

Jesus is truly awesome! He left Heaven and the Father to come to earth, be tortured and killed, for us. He came to heal broken hearts and deliver people who were bound. He came to give spiritual and physical sight to the blind and freedom to those who were wounded and held captive. But most importantly, Jesus came to give us eternal life. He came to be the propitiation for our sins. What an awesome God we serve!

Are you serving Jesus? Have you accepted His generous free gift of eternal life by becoming born again? Have you made Jesus the Lord of *your* life? If you cannot say yes to all these questions, change that right now. Give Jesus full reign in your life. Receive what He died to give you and start over fresh and new in Christ. Jesus died for the whole world; but only those who receive Him, receive salvation and eternal life.

Repeat this prayer: "Father I realize that I have sinned against you. I give You all rights to my life and ask that Jesus be my personal Lord and Savior. I accept His death and resurrection for my salvation. I want the Holy Spirit to fill me and lead me. Jesus died that I might have life and have it more abundantly. I receive abundant blessings in my life. Thank you, Father. In Jesus name I pray. Amen."

# YOU ARE COMPLETE NOW

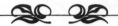

*For in Him dwelleth all the fullness of the Godhead bodily. And ye are complete in Him, which is the head of all principality and power.*

—Colossians 2:9, 10

We are complete in Jesus. He is the fullness of the Godhead. He dwells in us when we make Him our Lord. Therefore, if you've made Jesus your Lord, you lack no good thing. Yes, I realize that can be hard to believe sometimes. Especially, when we feel as though we are far from being complete in Him. Well, that is when you must exercise your faith. If God said it, then that settles it—no if, ands or buts about it.

You are complete in Christ Jesus! Knowing that, you must act like a complete person. Another person or a thing does not make you complete. You were made by God. Once you receive Jesus, you have everything you need. Couples oftentimes make the big mistake of entering into a relationship thinking that they need the other person to make them complete. That is not true. Each person in the relationship should be complete in Christ, self-sustaining and whole before connecting with another. Only God can complete you.

The Holy Spirit will help you walk in completeness. Only God can change you and make you into the whole person He created you to be. We cannot do it ourselves and neither can another person do it for us. Let God, through the Holy Spirit work out in you the fullness of your personality and abilities so you can be all He created you to be. "It is He who has made us and not we ourselves" (Psalms 100:3).

# IT'S TIME TO REST

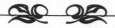

*Come unto me, all ye that labour and are heavy laden, and I will
give you rest. Take my yoke upon you, and learn of me; for I am
meek and lowly in heart; and ye shall find rest unto your souls.
For my yoke is easy, and my burden is light.*

—Matthew 11:28-30

If we are going to have peace, and enjoy our lives, we must
rest in God. The truth of the matter is that we will never have
peace or joy if it depends upon all our circumstances being
perfect. That just isn't going to happen. We must find our peace
and joy in God who changes not. People change, circumstances
change, things break and life has many surprises and storms.

Jesus said His yoke is easy and His burden is light. He wants
to take your heavy yoke, the one that is pulling you down to the
ground, and give you His light one that lifts you up. He wants
you to give Him the burden that is weighing you down and has
you bent over so He can remove it with His anointed power. I
think that's a pretty good exchange, don't you?

If you really want to enjoy your life and have unspeakable
joy in your heart, you must go beyond this physical, natural
world we live in and begin to live in the spiritual by putting your
trust in God. There is no lasting joy or peace apart from God.
Even if we manage to pull out a good day every now and then,
it will not be long before something comes along to put another
yoke around our necks to bring us down again.

Enter into the rest of God by giving Him your yokes and
burdens. Cast the care on Him. Know that God is going to see
you through and praise Him now for it. Then go out and enjoy
your day.

21

# AMAZING GRACE

*And He said unto me, My grace is sufficient for thee: for my strength is made perfect in weakness. Most gladly therefore will I rather glory in my infirmities, that the power of Christ may rest upon me.*

—2 Corinthians 12:9

saw God's grace most profoundly when my son was suddenly gone from this world. There was no way in the natural world that I could handle something as traumatic as that. My body and mind wanted to die and stop functioning. I could feel myself trying to shut down. But there was another stronger force working inside of me. That force was the Holy Spirit of God and He gave me the grace to withstand and hold up under unbearable circumstances. I did not lose my mind or physically break down. It was God's grace that pulled me through.

God's grace is not only prevalent in difficult situations, it is poured out to us daily. God gives us grace to do our jobs, to raise our children, to be good spouses, to be kind to irritating people, to serve in ministry and to live our everyday lives.

God has an unlimited amount of grace. If we are going to make it each day, we must receive more grace, especially in areas where we know we are weak. God will help us in our weakness if we receive His grace. We cannot handle this thing called life by ourselves. We need God and we need His power. Grace is power. It will not be given to us recklessly or when we do not need it. We are going to have to start depending on, specifically asking for, and receiving God's grace. God Himself told us in His Word, "Let us therefore come boldly unto the throne of grace, that we may obtain mercy and find grace to help in time of need" (Hebrews 4:16).

God will never let us get to a place where we don't need Him. He will always allow an area of weakness so you will have to rely on Him. Be thankful for your weaknesses. It gives God an opportunity to pour out His grace on you and let you experience His goodness and love.

# THANK GOD FOR HIS SUSTAINING POWER

*I laid me down and slept; I awaked; for the Lord sustained me.*
—Psalms 3:5

*I* thank God for waking me up this morning and starting me on my way. I rejoice every morning because it is only by God's grace that I see another day.

In case you did not know it, there is an enemy who is out to kill you. If he had his way, you would not have awakened this morning. He would have snuffed you out in your sleep last night. But glory to God, the enemy doesn't have his way and God kept you through the night and woke you up. As a matter of fact, He has been waking you every morning of your life! That is why each morning you should thank and praise God for another day. There is always someone, somewhere, who did not make it to see this day, but God gave you one more opportunity to fulfill the purpose He created you to accomplish.

Another benefit of giving praise to God right after waking up is that you start your day in a joyful mood. When you praise the Lord for His goodness, it is hard to be grumpy afterward. The world would be a much nicer place if people started their mornings thanking God for all the good things He has done in their lives.

Start today and every day hereafter, thanking God for His goodness and mercy. Thank Him for waking you up today. It is only by His mercy and grace that you made it through yesterday and last night. I believe that if you spend more time being grateful for all that God has done for you, you will not have time to dwell on the few things you do not have or the things that are not going quite the way you want them to. God has really been good to you and you can't thank Him enough.

# IS ANYTHING TOO HARD FOR THE LORD?

*The things which are impossible with men are possible with God.*
—Luke 18:27

The story of Abraham and Sarah having a baby is one of the most faith-increasing stories in the Bible. God took one-hundred-year old Abraham and ninety-year old Sarah and gave them the child they had prayed for all their lives. When the Lord told Abraham he would have a son, Sarah overheard and laughed within herself (Genesis 18: 10-12). But the Lord, who knows all things, asked why Sarah laughed and said, "Is anything too hard for the Lord?" (Genesis 18:14).

God is able. There is absolutely nothing that is impossible for God. However, human beings are limited, and there will be things that are impossible for you. Those things will remain impossible for you until you turn them over to the One who can handle the impossible.

God likes it when He gets to show off. He is looking for impossible situations to show Himself strong. If you have an impossible situation, then you are a prime candidate for a miracle from God. Throughout the Bible, God would wait until the situation was impossible before He stepped in so that everybody would know it was the true and living God who fixed the problem. That is all God wants to do in your life. He wants you and everybody who knows you to give Him the glory when He fixes your impossible situation.

If you are in need of a miracle today—don't be proud. Fall on your knees before God and receive it. It is there for you—all you have to do is ask and watch God do the impossible for you!

# PRESS TOWARD YOUR FUTURE

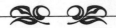

*Brethren, I count not myself to have apprehended: but this one thing I do, forgetting those things which are behind, and reaching forth unto those things which are before, I press toward the mark for the prize of the high calling of God in Christ Jesus.*

—Philippians 3:13-14

*H*olding on to the past keeps a lot of people from enjoying today and from having a good tomorrow. It is imperative that we leave the past behind us and move forward. Satan has used the failures, heartbreaks and mistakes of the past to instill fear and bitterness in many of us so we cannot move forward toward our future.

If this is happening to you, it's time to let the past go and press toward the mark of your bright future. You cannot change the past. What happened to you way back then, or even fifteen minutes ago, is over. Whether you will enjoy your life today and move toward a better tomorrow is determined by your "forgetting those things which are behind and reaching forth unto those things which are before." You must move on. You must choose to forget the bad events of the past and recognize that today is a new beginning filled with the promise of good things and blessings.

Remember, not everything in your past is bad. There is a lot more that is good when you weigh it out and you should focus on that. Today gives you another opportunity to create even more good, so take advantage of it. When Satan comes around trying to remind you of your past, just remind him of his future—an eternity of burning in the bottomless pit of Hell. I'll bet he won't be bringing up your past so quickly then.

Press on toward your glorious future with God and leave the past behind.

# TURN UP THE LIGHT

*Let your light so shine before men, that they may see your good works, and glorify your Father, which is in heaven.*

—Matthew 5:16

If you are a born-again believer who loves the Lord, people should know it. You should act and speak differently. You should handle problems differently. You should be making a difference everywhere you go. Your light should shine before men and you should be doing good works for the Lord so that He is glorified. Are you? If not, that can change today.

God is looking for people who will let their lights shine in this day and age. People are walking around in darkness and are looking for the light. If Jesus lives in you, then you have the light that they desperately need. But if the light is hidden, they will not be able to find Jesus—their only hope. Jesus said, "I am the light of the world: he that followeth me shall not walk in darkness, but shall have the light of life" (John 8:12).

If God has blessed you with His light, you must bless someone else with the light. God is depending on you to share it. Glorify God today by letting your light shine before men. Do good works and walk in the Spirit of God. Love other people. Let the joy of the Lord bubble out of you everywhere you go. You will find that as you share your light, it will get brighter and brighter. Keep on shining until your light is so bright the enemy is blinded by it and cannot get near you, while people who are searching for it will easily find it. Now go out and shine.

# YOU HAVE TRIUMPHED OVER THE WORLD

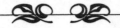

*Who is he that overcometh the world, but he that believeth that Jesus is the Son of God?*

—1 John 5:5

*I*n case you didn't know it, you are an overcomer. Yes, if you have made Jesus the Lord of your life, you have overcome the world. Well, you ask, what exactly does that mean? It means that anything the devil throws at you or in any trial or storm life brings your way, you have the power in you to overcome and be victorious.

There is nothing too big for you and God to handle. You can be victorious in everything you face. However, whether or not you will see the victory is up to you. Gaining the victory that God gives is based on your faith in God and His Word and your lifestyle of obedience and practical application of the Word. That is why Satan tries so hard to steal the Word from you as soon as it is planted in your heart. He knows that if you start living the Word you heard and believing it, you will defeat him every time. Don't let the devil steal the Word from you. You are going to be tested in the very area you are trying to get victory. Satan hopes it causes you to faint and quit believing. But God is using the test to build your faith and cause you to have deep roots that cannot be easily pulled up. "Knowing this, that the trying of your faith worketh patience. But let patience have her perfect work, that ye may be perfect and entire, lacking nothing" (James 1:3, 4).

So whether you need victory in your finances, your health, relationships or your faith itself, stand fast, be unmovable. Put the Word to work and pass the test. You will overcome.

# DON'T BLOCK YOUR BLESSINGS

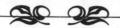

*A faithful man shall abound with blessings.*

—Proverbs 28:20

We all want to be more abundantly blessed. We all should want to be in the "above and beyond what we could ask or think" category of blessings. Well, according to this scripture, it is totally up to you. Your faithfulness is what will cause your blessings to abound. How faithful to God are you? Could it be that you are the one holding back your blessings by your lack of faithfulness? Hmm.

Most people view God as someone who sits up in Heaven and selectively picks out people to bless. They feel they are not blessed because God has skipped over them. Just like the lottery, their number hasn't come up yet. That is not how God works. God has given everybody the same tools to have victory and blessings in their lives. He has written them down and made them plain. He has given us teachers and preachers to help us understand and He's given us the Holy Spirit to reveal the truth to us.

God is not a respecter of person (Acts 10:34). He does not favor one person over another. Each of us has the same opportunity to receive salvation, deliverance and blessings as the other. What causes some to be blessed more than others is their faithfulness in developing a close relationship with God, studying and understanding His Word, which teaches us how to live a victorious life.

Your blessings are waiting on you. All that you desire is available. Get faithful with your commitment to God. It's time to stop playing around. Blessings are right around the corner.

 29

# TO KNOW BETTER IS TO DO BETTER

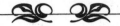

*Therefore to him that knoweth to do good, and doeth it not, to him it is sin.*

—James 4:17

I've noticed that people who are lost, without the knowledge of God, don't even seem to realize that sinful behavior is wrong. Sin has become so commonplace in their lives they don't even recognize it as sin.

Once we receive revelation from God about a sin in our lives, we are to repent and turn away from it. If we knowingly continue to engage in the sinful behavior, then to us it is sin. That is why God gave the Ten Commandments. The children of Israel did not know that their behavior was sinful. God had Moses write the law down so they could read it and become aware of their sin. However, God knew that we could not keep the law and would break it. Therefore, He sent His Son, Jesus, to be our Redeemer.

Now don't go out and stone yourself if you have sinned. Thank God that your sin bothers you. There was a time in your life that it didn't. Thank God that He loves you enough to convict you of sin so you can change. He will always forgive you. But you don't want to continue to do wrong once you know better. So pray that you are delivered from the sin forever. God is the only one who has the power to completely deliver you. So stay the course. Sometimes, it will take a while. Other times, it is instant and you never are tempted to engage in that sin again. Either way, you are on the road to conforming to the image of God.

Be thankful for the conviction of sin. To know better is to do better. Once you've been delivered, help someone else. Don't ever look down your nose at those who have not gotten their revelation or who are still struggling with sin. Pray for them, just as someone prayed for you. God will reveal it to them in His perfect timing. Meanwhile, just concentrate on yourself, because until we get to Heaven, we will always have imperfections and sin issues. But thanks be to God, He doesn't see us as sinners. And because we've been washed by the blood of Jesus, we can hold our heads high and know that God loves us just as we are. "There is therefore now no condemnation to them who are in Christ Jesus, who walk not after the flesh, but after the Spirit" (Romans 8:1).

# JUST BELIEVE

*And He said unto me, Son of man, can these bones live?*
*And I answered, O Lord God, thou knowest.*

—Ezekiel 37:3

*O*ur God is a God of restoration and resurrection. If there are some dead situations going on in your life, there is hope for resurrection in Christ! It doesn't matter if the situation is so dead there is nothing left but the bones. Remember that Lazarus had been dead for four days! Even his sister, Martha, said to Jesus, "Lord, by this time he stinketh." But Jesus calmly replied, "Said I not unto thee, that, if thou wouldest believe, thou shouldest see the glory of God? (John 11:39-40). Then Jesus went on to raise Lazarus from the dead.

I've got great news for you—Jesus Christ is the same yesterday, today and forever! He is still in the resurrection business. He still has the same resurrection power. He can raise your dead situation today, if you would believe. Have you given up? Have you thrown in the towel? You will never have restoration or resurrection if you don't believe you can have it. Do you think your situation has been dead for too long and is already stinking? Remember, there is nothing too hard for the Lord.

Renew your faith in God. Focus your mind on Jesus, not on your dead situation. Choose life. Life in Christ Jesus has the power to resurrect. God wants to restore unto you what the devil has killed, stolen and destroyed. It is never too late. Don't ever give up. As long as you have God, you have hope.

# THERE'S HOPE FOR TOMORROW

*Nevertheless we, according to His promise, look for new heavens and a new earth, wherein dwelleth righteousness.*

—2 Peter 3:13

*G*od keeps all His promises. He cannot lie. Everything that He says will be—will be. Therefore, we know that there will be a new Heaven and a new earth where no evil will exist. Satan will be cast into the lake of fire along with all his demons, and we will live in peace without sin. "And God shall wipe away all tears from their eyes: and there shall be no more death, neither sorrow, nor crying, neither shall there be any more pain; for the former things are passed away" (Revelation 21:4). Whew, I feel like shouting!

God knows that sometimes we just need to know that trouble does not last always. We need to have something to look forward to and dream about. We need to know that we win in the end. So He gives us this wonderful promise of eternal peace, righteousness and joy. What a wonderful Father He is.

Brothers and sisters just hold on. You have been given many precious promises for today and tomorrow. You have been guaranteed victory today and given hope for tomorrow. Don't give up now. It won't be long. You can have a new heaven right now on earth if you believe.

# MERCY, MERCY, MERCY

*It is because of the Lord's mercies that we are not consumed,*
*because His compassions fail not. They are new every morning:*
*great is thy faithfulness.*

—Lamentations 3:22-23

You know, if it were up to the devil, you would be consumed right now. He is constantly going before the Lord to tell Him all the awful, sinful things you do. But thank God for new mercy every day! He only sees the blood of Jesus that covers you. And when we repent of our sins, the Bible says that "He is faithful and just to forgive us our sins, and cleanse us from all unrighteousness" (1 John 1:9).

One of God's great characteristics is His compassion. He is so full of unconditional love that no matter what we do, He has mercy on us and His compassion never fails. He forgives and forgets the sins. The Bible says, "As far as the east is from the west, so far hath he removed our transgressions from us" (Psalms 103:12). That's some kind of forgiveness.

We should thank God every day for His mercy. His mercy endureth forever. He gives us brand-new mercy every day. Mercy means not getting what you deserve. We deserve death. Yep, you read me right—death. "For the wages of sin is death" (Romans 6:23a). Have you ever sinned? Thought so. Well, thank God for His mercy. Because the verse goes on to say, "But the gift of God is eternal life through Jesus Christ, our Lord", (Romans 6:23b). Instead of death, we get eternal life.

I am sure that burns the devil up—literally and figuratively!

*Norma DeShields Brown*

He can't stand the fact that God simply forgives us and sees us as righteous because of the blood shed by Jesus. That is why you *must* be covered under the blood of Jesus. It is the only thing that will keep you from spiritual death and Hell.

Thank you Jesus for the blood and your everlasting mercy.

# THE HARVEST IS READY

*God shall bless us; and all the ends of the earth shall fear Him.*

—Psalms 67:7

This is a great time to be alive and born again. We are living at a critical time in the church age where all prophecy must be fulfilled. God's Holy Spirit is going to flood the earth, and we who are His shall reap all the harvest of seeds sown for hundreds of years. We are about to be blessed like never before, and the world will know that God is good.

If I were you, I would sow as much seed as I could get into the kingdom right now. Your harvest will start to come up as soon as you plant it because the Bible says, "Behold, the days come, saith the Lord, that the plowman shall overtake the reaper, and the treader of grapes him that soweth seed; and the mountains shall drop sweet wine, and all the hills shall melt" (Amos 9:13). I'm telling you, you will reap a harvest before you even get the seed in the ground. Sow, sow, and sow some more. God is trying to bless you.

You are going to be blessed, child of God. However, you are going to be blessed in order to be a blessing and to glorify God. It is not so that you can boast and be greedy. So get your heart right before God now. Start giving. That makes you a prime candidate to receive the greatest harvest ever. Then get ready to receive the harvest, pressed down, shaken together and running over.

Welcome to Niles District Library!
- www.nilesdistrictlibrary.com
- 269-683-8545

You checked out the following items:

1. Joy comes this morning
   Barcode: 33006100202447
   Due: 8/2/12 11:59 PM
2. Bible therapy : how the Bible solve
   Barcode: 33007000001194
   Due: 8/2/12 11:59 PM

NDL-1 2012-07-12 15:43
Thank you Kathy Mankowski
Join us for Summer Reading!
June 4-July 28th.

# YOU AIN'T SEEN NOTHING YET

*Call unto me, and I will answer thee, and shew thee great and mighty things, which thou knowest not.*

—Jeremiah 33:3

*Y*ou haven't seen anything yet. God is ready to show us some things that we have not seen or known before. God is waiting to show us mighty things greater than the parting of the Red Sea, greater than the raising of Lazarus from the grave or Jesus walking on water. Glory to God!

We are living in a time when God's Spirit is being poured out like never before. Those who are willing to believe and step out on faith shall see great and mighty things which they "knowest not." God is showing Himself strong and bringing in the harvest of lost souls. If we will begin to call on the name of Jesus in faith and with authority, He will answer.

Take the limits off God. He has unlimited power, wealth, miracles and blessings. You need to believe in big things because we serve a big God. We should also pray big prayers. Why can't we eradicate racism, gangs, poverty and other big issues in this nation? Why can't we pray for peace in the Middle East? We serve a big and mighty God who can do all things. Pray in the spirit for the blessings that are exceeding abundantly, above all that you can ask or think (Ephesians 3:20). God is able to perform anything.

The Word says in 1 Corinthians 2:9, "Eye hath not seen, nor ear heard, neither have entered into the heart of man, the things which God hath prepared for them that love Him." Like I said before— You ain't seen nothing yet.

# BEHOLD THE GLORY

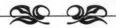

*But as truly as I live, all the earth shall be filled with the glory of the Lord.*

— Numbers 14:21

We are living in the time when the earth shall be filled with the glory of the Lord. We can start the process if we begin to allow the Holy Spirit to fill us and show the glory of God in our own lives. When we allow Him to take over and have His way, the glory of the Lord will shine on us. We will have a glow that is noticeable to all the world! The joy of the Lord will come through and actually show forth on your face. I've seen it in myself and others who have come to the place in their relationship with God where they have stopped looking at their circumstances and started looking to Jesus. You can't help but be filled with joy when you look to Jesus. You can't help but have hope when you look to Jesus and you can't help but shine when you are filled and flowing with His Spirit.

God's people are doing more now than ever before. God is pouring out His Spirit upon those who will receive it and walk in His commandments. You can't expect to receive the glory of God while walking in disobedience. So make a firm decision today and every day to give your all to Jesus. Can you just imagine what it will look like when all of God's children are filled with the glory of God and shining all over the place? The glory will be so much that the devil won't be able to see you for the light.

# YOU ARE PRESERVED

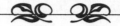

*The Lord shall preserve thy going out and thy coming in from this time forth, and even for evermore.*

*D*id you know that you have an around-the-clock body-guard? You do, in case you didn't know it. Almighty God has His eye on you 24-7 and He knows your comings and goings. He has angels that are encamped around you day and night. He sees everything you do and knows every thought that you think. He lives on the inside of you so you are never separated from Him—never! Now that's pretty deep when you think about it, isn't it?

God acts like an umbrella for you. He covers you from the rain that Satan tries to pour on you all day long. However, when you sin, it is as though you have stepped out from under the umbrella and now you're liable to get wet, struck by lightning, or hit by hail. You will remain uncovered until you repent. You do not ever want to be uncovered. Satan is just waiting for you to mess up and give him an opportunity to get you. The longer you leave yourself out, the more chances you allow the enemy. If you are feeling uncovered, get right with God and get back under the umbrella of His protection.

God has you in His hands. He has all your days numbered and knew you even before you were formed in your mother's womb. Knowing that God has you preserved should give you a sense of peace and comfort. You do not have to be afraid of things happening in the world. You are protected. "A thousand shall fall at thy side, and ten thousand at thy right hand, but it shall not come near thee" (Psalms 91:7).

Go out and enjoy today and every day. God is watching over you!

# ENJOY THE JOURNEY

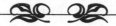

*Not that I speak in respect of want; for I have learned, in whatever state I am, in this to be content.*

—Philippians 4:11

*C*ontentment is something most of us think we will never have. We live in a world where we are always coming up with new and improved things. As soon as we reach a goal to get one thing, something better has been invented and now we need to set a new goal to get that. It seems that we are never satisfied. We want what everybody else has and everybody wants what we have. It is as if we are on a hamster's wheel, going around and around, never getting to that place of satisfaction.

I will tell you this, if you are waiting until you have everything you want and all your circumstances are perfect, you might as well forget contentment. Contentment is an inner decision to be satisfied wherever you are. It does not mean that you are to stop having goals and desiring to improve your status in life, but rather, you appreciate where God has you right now, while you're on your way to where you're going. You are satisfied because you have Jesus and all things are possible with Him. That's contentment, which leads to joy and peace.

While you are praying for things to change in your life, be content with where you are right now. You are right where God has called you to be at this time. We don't just go from cradle to palace. There is a process of getting there. You will get there if you remain steadfast. However, I believe you will get there a lot faster if you are grateful and content along the way. The children of Israel took forty years to make an eleven-day trip. All along the way they complained and murmured against God, which kept them out there forty years. Don't keep yourself from reaching your goals because of the same thing. Be thankful for where you are right now and what you already have. Enjoy the ride from where you are now to where you are going. You just might get there faster and with peace and joy in your heart, to boot.

# THE WORLD CAN WAIT

*Set your affection on things above, not on things on the earth.*

—Colossians 3:2

What a good piece of advice Paul gave to the church in Colosse. Then and now, the body of believers who comprise "The Church," had to be reminded that we are dead to the things of this world. Therefore, we should be much more concerned about the things of God than the things of this temporary world.

Have you noticed it is so easy to get caught up in the things of the world? There never seems to be enough time to get everything done. We end up spending less and less time with God in prayer, bible study and worship. Yet, those are the things we *must* make time for. They are the main things. It is hard to operate in harmony and have success without checking into headquarters each day and putting God first. When you have taken the time to check in with The Master, The Chief Executive Officer, before starting your day, you will have less stress and anxiety when the cares of this world try to swallow you up. He will comfort and calm like no other.

Start your day putting God first and setting your affection on Him. "Seek ye first the kingdom of God and His righteousness, and all these things shall be added unto you" (Matthew 6:33). All the things the world has, God will provide for you, if you'll seek Him. He knows you have need and want of those things. He will also give you the desires of your heart, but first you must delight yourself in the Lord (Psalms 37:4). We don't have to lust after the things of the world. Seek God and He will gladly give them to you. Set your affections above. You'll be blessed beyond measure.

# GOD WILL SPEAK TO YOU

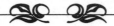

*Then Eli answered and said, Go in peace: and the God of Israel grant thee thy petition that thou has asked of him.*

—1 Samuel 1:17

It is such a wonderful experience to pray and get an answer from God regarding your petition. You have been praying diligently, pouring your heart out to God and then in your spirit you hear, "Go in peace, I will grant thee thy petition that thou has asked." You start to shout, praise, dance and shout some more because you know God has heard your cry and will come through. No devil in Hell will be able to make you doubt. No outward contradiction will make you waver. You've heard from God.

Sometimes we need to hear directly from God. It is good to hear from someone else that God will do what He said He would do. But sometimes you need to hear Him tell *you* He will do it for *you*. God can speak directly into your spirit the word you need to hear. He can speak His word in several ways. He can speak through your Pastor or Priest. Sermons are not for our entertainment. They are for edifying our spirits and to get a word from God. Have you ever noticed it seemed like the sermon was spoken directly to you, about your situation?

God can speak to you in His written Word—The Bible. The Holy Bible is God in written form. "In the beginning was the Word and the Word was with God, and the Word was God" (John 1:1). Your word is in The Word. Take the time to read it and study for yourself.

I recently got a huge revelation while watching a Pastor on television. He said that since God is the Word, when we speak the Word, we have actually heard from God. Did you get that? You have the Word you need to hear in you. You are an ambassador of Christ. So when you speak His Word, you are actually hearing from God Himself! So when you say, "By His stripes I am healed" (Isaiah 53:5, 1 Peter 2:24) you are hearing God speak to you through your own mouth. If I were you, I'd be speaking the Word every day. It has the power to change anything.

# A NEW LEASE ON LIFE

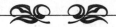

*And no man putteth new wine into old bottles, else the new wine doth burst the bottles, and the wine is spilled, and the bottles will be marred; but new wine must be put into new bottles.*

—Mark 2:22

With each new year people make many new resolutions. These goals or plans are things that we really want to do, but have not for one reason or another. We make a new commitment to start fresh and complete the task—for sure this time. However, most of those resolutions never come to completion. Somewhere down the line we quit, tucker out or never get started. What happens? Why can't we reach our goals and dreams? What is really going on?

I don't think most people take into consideration the full range of changes that need to be made when taking on a new direction. It is easy to set the goal, but difficult to do the daily activities that will make the goal a reality. In other words, we try to have a different outcome, but still want to do the same things the same way. We are trying to put new wine into old bottles. The new wine is the goal—lose weight, start a business, go back to school, pray and read the Bible every day. The old bottle is snacking, not exercising, making excuses, sleeping late, etc. We cannot put the new wine—goal—into the old bottle—old habits and ways. In order to make the goal a reality this year, you are going to have to start with new bottles.

You cannot achieve different results and still do the same things. You must change your thinking and your behaviors. It might also mean—depending on the goal—changing friends and relationships. You are a new creature in Christ. Your old self—bottle—is dead. Old things have passed away. Behold, today all things are new. Start with the inner you. How you think about yourself is critical to your success. "For as he thinketh in his heart, so is he"(Proverbs 23:7). Erase and destroy all those negative thoughts of yourself. See yourself on the other side of the goal. Know who you are in Christ and act accordingly. You can do all things through Christ who strengthens you. Do not listen to people who discourage you. Listen to God and make Him your accountability partner.

This is your year! You are stepping into the exceedingly, abundantly above and beyond realm. I am believing in you and God is, too.

# YOU ARE INVITED TO A WEDDING

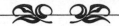

*Let us be glad and rejoice, and give honor to him; for the marriage of the Lamb is come, and his wife hath made herself ready.*

—Revelation 19:7

If you've ever been to a big wedding, you know how beautiful they can be. The flowers, decorations, candles, not to mention the food and drinks—can be something straight out of a movie. Well, the most elaborate and expensive wedding you can imagine is nothing compared to the one you're about to be invited to—the marriage of the lamb. But get this—not only are you invited—you are the bride!

When you made Jesus the Lord of your life and received the gift of salvation, you became engaged to Jesus. This engagement says that Jesus Himself wants to be with you forever and ever and take care of all your needs. This engagement is a binding covenant that cannot be broken. Jesus is not like a mortal man. He will not break your heart or call off the wedding. He keeps all His promises—not one of them is broken. And men, you are considered the bride, too.

Don't miss the wedding. This is not one of those situations where you can just show up for the reception. This wedding is private and unless you have a personal invitation, you cannot get in. Once everyone with an invitation is in, the door is closed. How wonderful it is to be invited to this wedding. "Blessed are they who are called unto the marriage supper of the Lamb" (Revelation 19:9).

The invitation is extended to you. God is awaiting your

RSVP. Will you accept and spend eternity with the Lord, or regretfully decline and spend eternity in Hell? The choice is yours. Put it this way—the Lord of Lords, King of Kings, maker of the earth and all therein, has just asked you to marry Him. Will you say yes? I pray so. I look forward to seeing you at the wedding.

# BE PROUD OF WHO YOU ARE

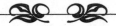

*For I am not ashamed of the gospel of Christ; for it is the power of God unto salvation to everyone that believeth; to the Jew first, and also to the Greek.*

—Romans 1:16

*Let* the redeemed of the Lord say so. We should never be ashamed of the gospel. It is the gospel that leads to salvation. In the gospel is so much power, that it literally transforms our inner man from darkness into light. Don't hide the fact that you are a child of God—saved, born-again and living for God. Be proud of who you are and hold your head up high. You are born into a royal priesthood by adoption. That adoption cost a whole lot. Jesus had to be crucified on the cross so you could come into the family.

As a child of God, you will not always fit in. That is to be expected. We are no longer of the world. If we talk, act and think like the world how will anyone know we are from a different family? Who will we be able to influence for God and His kingdom? No one. Your walk should match your talk and both should represent the Lord.

When others begin to see that you are serious in your relationship with the Lord, they will respect you, if nothing else. It may even influence their behavior. They may not curse or gossip around you. They may feel uncomfortable telling dirty jokes in your presence. They might even come to you for advice when problems arise.

Be proud to be a Christian. Not just in word, but also in deed. Actions do speak louder than words. Your life may be the only Bible someone can read. Stand up, be proud and say so.

# CHANGE REQUIRES KNOWLEDGE

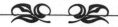

*That ye might walk worthy of the Lord unto all pleasing, being fruitful in every good work, and increasing in the knowledge of God.*
—Colossians 1:10

As Christians, we should desire to be more like Christ. That is after all, what Christian means—to be Christ-like; followers of Christ. For the vast majority of us, it will mean major change. However, it is change for the better and we should welcome it. If we do not change, we will never walk worthy of the Lord and please Him. Jesus is worthy of our very best effort to please Him every day. He made the ultimate sacrifice for us—His life—and the least we can do is offer ourselves as a living sacrifice.

How then, do we, who are so unworthy, walk worthy of the Lord? Colossians 1:9 tells us how. "That ye might be filled with the knowledge of his will in all wisdom and spiritual understanding." We must take it upon ourselves to know God's will and get understanding of His Word. This increases our knowledge of God. To know God is to love God and you will want to walk worthy of the Lord when you know Him. You must have a personal and intimate relationship with the Lord. Spend time with God every day. This is where we begin to receive spiritual wisdom and understanding. The Holy Spirit that is in us imparts wisdom that we could not get otherwise. Then, go to church. You will gain even more wisdom and understanding from an anointed teacher of the Word. God has given these men and women to increase our knowledge of Him.

The ball is in your court. It is your move. You have no excuse. Are you willing to take up the cross and carry it? Do you want to walk worthy of the Lord and be all God has created you to be? Or do you want to continue in ignorance and struggle through life aimlessly, outside of the will of God, not bearing any good fruit? Things will never work for you this way. You will never have real joy until you line up with the will of God.

If you really want to please God, learn of Him and seek His will. Increase in your knowledge. "Get wisdom, get understanding.... Wisdom is the principal thing; therefore, get wisdom; and with all thy getting, get understanding" (Proverbs 4:5a, 7).

# LET GOD BECOME YOUR CEO

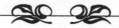

*I would seek unto God, and unto God would I commit my cause,
who doeth great things and unsearchable, marvelous things
without number.*

—Job 5:8, 9

It is no secret what God can do. His marvelous works are without number. He is able and willing to do exceedingly and abundantly more than what we ask Him for. He has more ways of blessing us than the human mind can conceive. That is why I love Him so much. He is so good and so awesome, I am just grateful that I know Him as my Father and Lord.

God promises that if we commit our way to Him, He will do unsearchable and great things for us. If you have a new or existing endeavor, the best thing you can do right now is to seek God and commit yourself and your project to Him. Let God become your permanent CEO. He will direct your paths and the outcome will always be success.

God also promises that He will bless the work of our hands when we honor Him. Always give God first place in your life. He knows the beginning from the end and will show you things only He can see. Our way will be much easier with God than without Him.

Commit everything you do unto God. He has ways of blessing you that are unsearchable. His ways are perfect, marvelous and never ending. If you were looking to hire someone to run your company, wouldn't you want someone who had a proven track record of never failing, always producing huge profits and was all-knowing, all-powerful and able to do the impossible? If such a person existed, they would cost you a fortune. However, you have just that in the Lord Jesus. He will guarantee you huge success and the best part is—He's free.

# DO YOU REALLY KNOW GOD?

*Know therefore, that the Lord thy God, He is God, the faithful God, who keepeth covenant and mercy with them who love Him and keep his commandments to a thousand generations.*

—Deuteronomy 7:9

There is one thing about God that is irrefutable. He is faithful and He cannot lie. He is who He says He is and He will do what He says He will do. But He will only be a myth until you try Him for yourself. You must "know therefore that the Lord thy God, he is God, the faithful God."

How would you know if a person you meet is trustworthy, honest and kind unless you spend some quality time with them and check them out? Well, the same goes for God. You must spend some quality time with Him to know for yourself that He is who He says He is. Put His Word into practice and expect to see results. Test Him and try Him. He doesn't mind. He Himself says, "Bring ye all the tithes into the storehouse, that there may be meat in mine house, and prove me now herewith, saith the Lord of hosts, if I will not open for you the windows of heaven, and pour out for you a blessing, that there shall not be room enough to receive it" (Malachi 3:10). He wants to show you how good, faithful, merciful and trustworthy He is.

God will always keep His covenant with you. He swore it to your forefathers. He keeps His word. He is the Faithful God. I can say that over and over until my face turns green. But until you try God for yourself, it will not make a bit of difference. You need to know. You need to trust Him. You must believe in Him.

I implore you to really take the time to know God. I can say for me, it has been the most rewarding and exciting relationship in the world. I had not been loved until I allowed Jesus to love me. I hadn't known unconditional love until Jesus gave it to me. It literally had no strings attached. Jesus is more than a friend. He is a Father, Brother, Husband, Doctor, Lawyer, Counselor, Comforter, all wrapped up in One. He is whatever you need Him to be. But don't take my word for it—try Him for yourself.

# THE GOLDEN RULE

*And as ye would that men should do to you, do ye also to them.*

—Luke 6:31

If we would just follow this one command, the world would be a wonderful place. If we always put ourselves in the other person's shoes, we would really think twice before doing some of the things we do to each other. But most times, we don't. We are by nature, selfish, self-centered, ungrateful and stingy. We have ourselves on our minds. Oftentimes, we don't think what would be best for the other person.

In order to follow the Golden Rule, we need to renew our minds. We must discipline ourselves to think first about the other person and how our actions will affect them before we act, say or do. Make that a commitment today. Before you act or speak, think about the other person it will affect. Put yourself into their shoes. Now ask yourself, would you want to be talked to that way? Would you want to be treated that way? Would you like it if that were done to you? It's really something to think about isn't it? It helps to remember that we always reap what we sow. Therefore, we need to pay closer attention to what seeds we sow each day. Sometimes we are going through hard places simply because of the seeds we have sown in the past.

God is very concerned with how we treat each other. He commands us to love one another as we love ourselves. In other words, do unto others as you would have them do unto you. It sounds so simple, yet it is very hard to put into minute-by-minute practice. So start practicing. It will take forced discipline, but we can do it, because God tells us to. He will never tell us to do something and not equip us to be able to do it.

Just think—all of us practicing the Golden Rule every day. We really could have world peace after all.

# The Love of God

# TRUE LOVE CANNOT BE SEPARATED

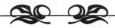

*For I am persuaded, that neither death, nor life, nor angels, nor principalities, nor powers, nor things present, nor things to come, nor height, nor depth, nor any other creature, shall be able to separate us from the love of God, which is in Christ Jesus our Lord.*
—Romans 8:38, 39

We've all probably felt at one time or another that God must be sick and tired of us. We've promised over and over again that we wouldn't do something, only to turn around and do the very thing we said we wouldn't do. We feel that we are not worthy to receive God's forgiveness one more time. Have you ever felt that way? I know I have. But thank God, He doesn't respond to us based on our feelings. He acts only on His Word.

The Apostle Paul expressed this truth in Romans 8:38-39. He said in essence that absolutely nothing could make God stop loving us. God's love is agape—pronounced a-gah-pay—love. This kind of love is not based on feelings but on choice. It doesn't change because of a person's actions; it remains constant and unconditional.

God loves you that way. He is no respecter of persons. He doesn't love the Apostle Paul or John the Baptist, Moses or even Jesus more than you. God is love, and He loves you completely and unconditionally just the way you are. Focus on that love. Close your eyes and say, "Father, I know you love me. Jesus loves me so much that He chose to die for me. I receive your love right now. Thank you, Lord. In Jesus name, Amen."

Let the love of God pour over you, around you and in you. Receive it by faith not by feeling. Just believe. And remember, there is absolutely nothing you can do that would ever separate you from the love of God.

# GOD CARES

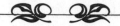

*Casting all your care upon Him; for He careth for you.*

—1 Peter 5:7

have often wondered what it would be like to live an entire day without any cares. I want to experience that someday, but, like most of you, I have a difficult time casting *all* my cares on God. I cast some of them, usually the big ones like bills I do not have the money to pay, health problems, business problems, people problems, etc. But the smaller ones I try to handle myself. What do I mean by smaller cares? Maybe you can relate to some of these. What should I have for dinner? I want to eat healthier, but it's so easy to pick up something fast and I do not feel like cooking. How much should I spend at the mall? I have a budget, but I must have that outfit that is over the budget — should I or shouldn't I just this once? Should I give the homeless man at the stoplight some money? I saw him at another stoplight last week. Is he really homeless or playing people? We are called to help the least of these. I just don't know.

God wants us to cast all our care upon Him. He even wants to take the care out of the routine tasks and decisions we have every day. God wants us to get to the place where we are totally leaning on Him for everything. Yes, He will even help you spend your money wisely and eat right. Just ask Him. The Bible says, "Ye have not because ye ask not" (James 4:2). I am determined to get to the place where I am casting all my care on God. I'm not there yet, but I am going to keep pressing toward that mark. I can only imagine the peace and joy that would come over me if I truly did not worry about anything.

Why don't you join me in making a committed effort to cast all your cares on God today? God can easily handle all your cares and concerns and still run the universe without breaking a sweat. I figure, if He wants to handle my cares, I should certainly give them to Him. I just thank God that He cares that much about me and you.

# YOU ARE SO BEAUTIFUL

*I will praise thee; for I am fearfully and wonderfully made:
marvelous are thy works: and that my soul knoweth right well.*
—Psalms 139:14

*f* you have ever felt bad about yourself, how you look, your body, or your personality, then this scripture is definitely the cure.

Just think about those words for a minute—"fearfully" and "wonderfully." The word fearfully means respectfully. When God put you together in His mind, He had major respect for your creation. He knew beforehand what He needed you to do in the earth. You are made the exact way He needed you to be. He never makes a mistake—not ever! So if you have big feet, it is because you need them for your purpose. If you have a handicap, God didn't make a mistake—He wants you to do wonderful things in spite of the handicap. He wants you to show the world that if I can, I know you can. That is how God gets glory.

God also made you wonderfully. The *American Heritage Dictionary* gives the definition of *wonderful* as capable of eliciting wonder; astonishing; admirable; excellent. God wants you to astonish the world. He created you to elicit wonder and to be admired. You were made in excellence and you are to be excellent. You are God's perfectly made child. The world has its own standards of beauty and success, but we are not part of the world. "Man looks at the outward appearance, but God looks at the heart" (1 Samuel 16:7). In God's eyes, you are beautiful. So you should see yourself the way God sees you—beautiful, righteous and wonderfully made!

# BE ENCOURAGED

*Remember His marvelous works that He hath done, His wonders, and the judgments of His mouth.*

—1 Chronicles 16:12

*M*y Pastor once preached a sermon about encouraging yourself. He taught us that when everyone had turned against King David, he reached down inside of himself and thought about God's goodness and all God had done for him, and he encouraged himself.

I dare you to think about God's marvelous works in your own life. Yes, you can read about all the wonderful miracles God did in the Bible, but if you have lived any length of time, you probably have a few personal miracles of your own you can refer to.

If by some unlikely chance you can't think of anything God has brought you through or done for you, then pick up the Bible and read the awesome things He has done for other people just like you. If your back is against the wall, read how God parted the Red Sea and allowed the children of Israel to cross over on dry land to escape the Egyptians (Exodus 14:14-30). If you are being persecuted for your beliefs and are being asked to compromise or give them up, read how God delivered the three Hebrew boys, Shadrach, Meshach and Abednego, from the fiery furnace without them even smelling like smoke (Daniel 3:20-27). If it doesn't seem your money is going to last until the next payday, then read about the multitude of over five thousand people Jesus fed with only five loaves of bread and two fish (Matthew 14:17-21). If you are sick in your body and need to be healed, turn to Mark 5:21-29, and read how He healed Jairus's daughter and the woman with an issue of blood. The Gospels of Matthew, Mark and Luke are filled with examples of complete deliverance from all sickness and disease.

No matter what your situation is God has got the problem covered. He is the same God today, and He will do the same things for you. Be encouraged.

# TELL GOD THANK YOU

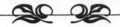

*Oh, give thanks unto the Lord; for He is good; for His mercy endureth forever.*

—1 Chronicles 16:34

The Bible tells us that we are to give thanks in everything (1 Thessalonians 5:18). Yes, even thank God when things are not going the way you would like them to. Do you know why? Because God is going to use the trials to refine us and make us as pure gold. Because of His great mercy toward us, He will not ever allow more to come upon us than we can bear. So if you are in a trial or when the next one comes, give thanks to God that He is changing you and refining your faith which is more precious than gold. "Wherein ye greatly rejoice, though now for a season if need be, ye are in heaviness through manifold temptations: that the trial of your faith, being much more precious than of gold that perisheth though it be tried with fire, might be found unto praise and honour and glory at the appearing of Jesus Christ" (1 Peter 1:6, 7).

Each of us needs to see how God works in our own lives, so we will know in every situation God is able.

Give thanks to God all day long. For waking you up, giving you shelter, providing for your daily needs, giving you food to eat and clothes to wear, caring for your family and friends, giving you a job or the one that's on the way, preserving your health, protecting you from evil, and dying for your salvation. The list can go on and on. Just begin to make it a habit to say "thank you." If we expect gratitude when we say or do something nice for others, how much more should we thank God, who is always good, gracious, kind, merciful, forgiving, faithful and loving toward us.

# YOU ARE AN HEIR

*The Spirit Himself beareth witness with our spirit, that we are the children of God: And if children, then heirs; heirs of God, and joint-heirs with Christ; if so be that we suffer with Him, that we may also be glorified together.*

—Romans 8:16, 17

If you are a born-again child of God—you have received Jesus as your Savior and Lord by confessing and believing that He is Lord according to Romans 10:9—you are an heir of Almighty God and a joint heir with Jesus Himself. As an heir, fully adopted with all legal rights into God's family, you have everything Jesus has, which is literally everything.

Maybe you find this hard to believe. Maybe you are thinking although this is true, you will not receive it until you get to Heaven. Wrong! Jesus died so that you could become a member of the family of God and receive the blessings now. In John 10:10, Jesus says that He came so we would have abundant life.

What would it benefit you if a long-lost relative left you a million dollars in their will, but you did not know it and no one told you? You would be entitled to it, and it would be legally yours, but you would not be able to experience the abundant life that million dollars could provide for you. And when you died and got to Heaven, that million dollars would not be of any use. Well, the same holds true for your inheritance from God. You need the blessings now, not in Heaven. You have been told that everything the Lord has is yours. Everything you need, He will provide. Take hold of your inheritance by faith. Faith is the passageway that brings the manifestation of your inheritance on earth—now.

John 10:9 says that the thief—Satan—comes to kill, steal and destroy. Satan will try to keep your inheritance from you. He lost all of his and now hates to see anyone receive theirs. But he can't stop you from getting it once you declare it's yours and have faith in God to receive it. Keep on believing God's Word. God never fails. You are His child. You are an heir.

# ARE YOUR NEEDS BEING MET?

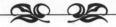

*According as His divine power hath given unto us all things that pertain unto life and godliness, through the knowledge of Him that hath called us to glory and virtue.*

—2 Peter 1:3

If you have a need today, God has given you whatever you need. Through Jesus, we have all our needs supplied. Jesus is our provider and supplier. Right now, take your need to the Lord. Ask Him so that you can receive. I really believe that many of us are going around with unmet needs because either we think that they are too small for God to work with, or we simply have forgotten that we have a Heavenly Father who loves us and wants to take care of us. God told us to give all our cares to Him because He cares for us (1 Peter 5:7).

God not only provides what we need, He also gives us every thing that pertains to living a godly life. If we truly love the Lord, we want to live right. But we cannot do it without the divine power of God working in our lives. We only frustrate ourselves when we try to live holy and be righteous on our own. It takes the power of the Holy Spirit to change us and work holiness in us.

The more knowledge you have about God, the more you will want to be like Him. Learn of Him and His ways and seek His kingdom first. Give your sin over to God also. He wants to cleanse you and help you to change. He can deliver you and set you free from any bondage. God will change you, take care of you, and bless you in a way you never could imagine.

# DADDY'S HOME

*The Lord also will be a refuge for the oppressed, a refuge in times of trouble. And they that know thy name will put their trust in thee: for thou, Lord, has not forsaken them that seek thee.*

—Psalms 9:9, 10

You may have to say this every day as a reminder to yourself, but God has not forsaken you. He loves you and will never leave you. That is a promise.

When times are hard, we sometimes feel as though God has left us alone. He hasn't. It is in the hard times that we must seek after God. We must not let our feelings keep us from the only One who can help us. God is our refuge and we must learn to put our trust in Him. When we talk to God about our trouble, He hears and comes to our rescue. God enjoys handling our problems and blessing us. He never gets tired of us coming to Him. He is our Daddy. Good daddies take care of their children and make sure they have everything they need. They come to our rescue when we are in trouble, and they admonish the people who are messing with us. Our Heavenly Daddy does much more than an earthly one. He can do what man cannot, so we should rely on Him.

Your Daddy will not let you down. He loves you too much. You can be confident that He will always be there to help you. If your child had a need and you were able to meet that need, would they have to beg you to help them? Absolutely not! Well, your Heavenly Daddy can meet your need. He is waiting for you to ask and trust. That's all. It's time to have a little talk with your Daddy.

# MMM, MMM GOOD

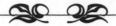

*Even every one that is called by my name: for I have created him for my glory. I have formed him; yea, I have made him.*

—Isaiah 43:7

The old folks use to say, "God don't make no junk." That is so true. Everything God made was good. In the book of Genesis, when God made the heavens, light, sun, and moon, He looked at it and saw that it was good.

"So God created man in His own image, in the image of God created He him; male and female created He them" (Genesis 1:27). Therefore, you, too, are created in the image of God. You are wonderfully and uniquely made. God made you in love. The Bible says that God is love (1 John 4:8), and He made you in His image, which is love. You are so loved by God that He gave His only begotten Son so that you could live and not perish (John 3:16). That kind of love is incomprehensible. Human minds cannot grasp it. It goes way over one's head. Just ask yourself this question: if mankind needed a sacrifice in order to save itself, and your child, your baby, was the only one who could do it, would you offer him or her up to be brutally murdered for people who do not even know you? That's deep, isn't it? Well, that is exactly what God did, because He loved you that much and wanted you to be in fellowship with Him and live with Him for all eternity. If you did not mean anything to God, then He gave His only Son for nothing. He loves you more than you will ever be able to understand.

God created you so that you would give Him glory. He needs

you to glorify Him in your walk, talk and thoughts. Work on that. God deserves your very best every single day. He made you to have huge success so that you can tell the world about Him. Always give Him all the honor and praise. We can do nothing apart from God—not even take another breath.

The best is yet to come for you. You are God's special creation and "God don't make no junk." Give God the praise!

# YOU'RE THE APPLE OF GOD'S EYE

*Keep me as the apple of the eye, hide me under the shadow of thy wings.*
—Psalms 17:8

Did you know that you are the apple of God's eye? You are. All of His children are the apple of His eye.

I have a saying that I recite from time to time. "I'm God's favorite child." I say that because I feel that way. I know that God loves us all with the same unconditional love. But when I am with God in prayer or worship, I truly feel as though I am His favorite at that very moment. I believe God wants me to feel that way. He enjoys me knowing that He loves me and that I am the apple of His eye.

God says that we are to come to Him as little children (Matthew 18:4). Doesn't a small child sitting on Daddy's lap feel as though he is the most special child in the house at that moment? God does not mind us feeling that way about ourselves. That is why it is important that we know who we are in Christ, and what God has to say about us. Otherwise, we will look to people to define who we are, and that can be disastrous.

Because you are the apple of God's eye, know that God is looking over you every moment of the day and He will protect you. God says that He will keep you under His wings (Psalms 91:4). Satan may come by roaring like a lion and try to devour you, but he will not be able to get to you while you are hidden away under the wings of the Almighty. He can only walk back and forth making a loud noise. The noise might give you a headache, but it won't kill you. So stay under your Father's wings where you will be protected and safe and God can keep His eye on you.

# ANGELS IN THE MIDST

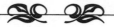

*There shall no evil befall thee, neither shall any plague come nigh thy dwelling. For he shall give his angels charge over thee to keep thee in all thy ways. They shall bear thee up in their hands, lest thou dash thy foot against a stone.*

—Psalms 91:10-12

*D*o you believe in angels? You should because the Bible confirms that angels do indeed exist. My personal testimony of angelic protection came early one morning after all-night prayer at my church. Returning home around 3 a.m., I slowly backed into my driveway to park in the garage. Once inside the garage, I looked up to see a car speeding into my driveway with what looked like three or four men inside. I quickly realized that I might be in trouble.

Two scenarios came to my mind. (1) I was about to be car-jacked. (2) I was about to be assaulted and robbed, maybe even raped. As I pushed the button on the remote to close the garage door, one of the men jumped from the backseat of the car and ran toward me. I knew that the garage door would immediately retract when the man ran across the sensor, and I panicked. Their vehicle was blocking mine, so I couldn't just put my foot on the gas and go. But as soon as the man reached the front of his vehicle, a look of horror came on his face and he immediately turned and jumped back in the car. The driver had the car in Reverse before the guy could close the door. The car sped backward so fast it almost hit the streetlight across from my house. They disappeared, leaving skid marks in the street. After closing the garage door and sitting there a minute to regroup, I looked around to see what had shaken them so. Was there someone in the garage? I did not see anything. I got out of the car and went into the house. I started praising and thanking God for my safety and immediately God put into my spirit that the men had been allowed to see my angels. That is what had frightened them off. I did not see them with my physical eyes, but the men did. Wow! I can only imagine what my angels must have looked like.

You have angels encamped all around you. So relax. They will not allow demons to run roughshod over you. Stand on God's Word and proclaim, no evil shall befall me, neither come near my dwelling. For God shall give His angels charge over me, to keep me in all my ways. Thank you, God, for my precious angels.

# GOD IS WITH YOU

*Have not I commanded thee? Be strong and of a good courage; be not afraid, neither be dismayed: for the Lord thy God is with thee whithersoever thou goest.*

—Joshua 1:9

There is never any time that God is not with you. He is always near to those who call Him Father. So stand firm and be confident because God is always with you wherever you go. You do not have to be afraid of your circumstances. They are not the truth. God's Word is the truth. If He made promises to you regarding those circumstances, then hold fast and believe. God is faithful. He will do what He said He would do.

God knows that sometimes fear will attack us. That is why He said, "Be not afraid." He wants us to look beyond the thing that is causing the fear and see Him. He does not want us to get dismayed because of how things may appear. His Word is our strengthener. Use it often. It will lift you up, encourage you, and enlighten you.

The Word has power. It is the most powerful weapon we have against the enemy. Fear is from the enemy. If Daniel could walk into a den of lions and not be afraid because he knew God was with him, you can walk into a bank and ask for a loan to start a business. The odds might be against you, but you have God. And just as those lions lost their hunger and went to sleep, the thing the enemy has sent to devour you will not succeed, either. God is always in control. He controls the enemy. Fear not. Be strong and of good courage. God is with you every step of the way.

# REMOVE ALL LIMITATIONS TODAY

*Jesus said unto him, If thou canst believe, all things are possible to him that believeth.*

—Mark 9:23

*A*ll things are possible with God. Do you believe that? If you do, then it is time to take the limits off your dreams, desires and requests to God. There is no limit to what God can do. If you can think it in your mind, God can do it. He created your mind, remember? He gave you the power to think and think *big*. God is not a small God. Look around you. He created the earth and everything in it. He created man with his extremely complex and awesome cellular structure from the dust of the ground. And you think your requests are too big for God? No way. You can't even think bigger than what God can do.

If God said to you, "There are absolutely no limits to what you can have in this life. What do you desire?" What would your answer be? Think about that and take some time to write the answer down. Remember, there are absolutely no limits on what you can ask God for. You do not have to limit your list to just finances and material things, either. Include spiritual, emotional, social and any other things you would like to have. The sky is the limit, so think *big!* Pray and seek God's will for your life.

When God asked this very question of King Solomon, "Ask what I shall give thee" (1 Kings 3:5), he said he wanted to have wisdom so he could judge rightly his people (1 Kings 3:9). When God saw his heart, He not only gave him what he asked for, He gave him wealth and riches too (1 Kings 3:11-14). When you ask according to His will, it shall be done.

Now, if you can believe and ask God for the things on that list, God says that He can bring them to pass because nothing is impossible with Him.

# GOD LOVES YOU

*And we have known and believed the love that God hath to us. God is love; and he that dwelleth in love dwelleth in God, and God in him.*

—1 John 4:16

It is imperative that we know how much God loves us. Even when our circumstances or feelings say otherwise, we know that God loves us so much that He gave His only Son to die for us.

I know at times it is hard for us to believe that God could or would love us that much. But He does. Sometimes when bad things happen to us, such as the death of a loved one or other tragic situations, we wonder how a loving God could let this happen. No one can answer the whys where God is concerned. He is sovereign and knows all things; we only know in part. If God allowed it to happen, then it will work together for our good (Rom. 8:28). We must trust Him and know that He would never do anything to intentionally hurt us. God is love and love is not cruel or evil. Satan is the culprit in all bad things. Our anger should always be directed toward him.

God wants to tell you "I Love You" today and every day. Many people who do not have a significant other or someone special in their lives, feel left out and lonely. People get depressed and think they are not loved. That is the furthest thing from the truth. You do not need a romantic relationship to have and experience true love. God loves you. God really loves you. Just because you cannot see Him or touch Him, does not mean He is not there. He is there more than any human person can be. He is there 24-7, 365 days of the year.

Do not allow the devil to convince you that because you do not have a man or woman to share your life with or if you do and things aren't going right, you are not loved. God loves you. Receive His love today.

# IT'S CHRISTMAS EVERY DAY WITH GOD

*If ye then, being evil, know how to give good gifts unto your children, how much more shall your Father, which is in Heaven give good things to them that ask Him?*

—Matthew 7:11

God is the ultimate Father. He birthed everything that exists in the world, and he knows everything about all that exists, including you. He knows everything about being a father because He is the Father of fathers. Think about that.

If we can be good to our children with a limited understanding of true and unconditional love, then how much more will our Heavenly Father, who is love, give us the things we ask for and need? Come on now.

We fail to realize that God takes pleasure in our prosperity. "Let them shout for joy, and be glad, that favour my righteous cause: yea, let them say continually, Let the Lord be magnified, which hath pleasure in the prosperity of His servant" (Psalms 35:27). God wants to bless us. Who else does He have to bless but His children? We have erroneously characterized God to be like us—fickle, unforgiving, mean, selfish, stingy—you get the picture. He is nothing like us. Even though we were created in His image, we never were on God's level; and after sin came into the world, we became sinful, evil and like the devil. It is not until we become born again that we can begin to be changed into the image of Christ.

God wants to bless you just because He loves you. He also wants to show the world how loving, good and generous He is to those who name Him Father and Lord. When others see how good your Father is to you—they will want Him to be their Father, too.

# YOU ARE BLESSED

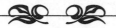

*I have been young, and now am old; yet have I not seen the righteous forsaken, nor his seed begging bread. He is ever merciful, and lendeth; and his seed is blessed.*

—Psalms 37:25, 26

God never forsakes the righteous. Not only that, you will always have bread and be blessed. It is a promise from God. Now if you honestly do not know if you are a child of God, you can become one right now, and immediately you will be counted as one of the righteous. Believe that the power of God has redeemed you from sin and death and made you a part of the righteousness of God in Christ Jesus. It is by faith that you are saved (Ephesians 2:8).

From now on, you never have to worry about your needs being met. The righteous—all who have called on the name of Jesus—will never be forsaken, nor will their seed, their children, have to beg for bread.

God knows your needs before you do. He will prepare you long before the need arises. You must listen and obey to what He is telling your spirit to do. So when you have the unusual desire to buy extra food or clothing and you have the resources to do so—do not go into debt, that's not God's way—pray and ask God about it. God could be preparing you for something that is coming your way. You could end up being like Joseph, who saved a whole nation because God had warned him that a famine was coming and he stored up. However, even if you miss God and fail to prepare, God will keep you in times of need and trouble. Always remember that and keep your peace. You have God's Word to assure you that you will never be forsaken, nor will your children be without. You are truly blessed.

# HIS EYE IS ON THE SPARROW AND YOU

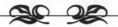

*Are not two sparrows sold for a farthing? And one of them shall
not fall on the ground without your Father. Fear not, therefore, ye
are of more value than many sparrows.*

—Matthew 10:29, 31

God will always take care of us. He adores and loves us
more than we will ever know or understand. Yet, we forget how
important we are to God. The Bible tells us that God feeds and
clothes the birds of the air and the lilies of the field, which do
not have nearly as much value as we do. So how much more
will He make sure that we are fed and clothed?

Recognize who you are. You are the son or daughter of the
living God, the Creator of the universe. You are God's child.
You were bought from the devil with the blood of God's only
Son, Jesus. Jesus suffered beyond human comprehension
when He did not have to, so that you and I could have a relationship with the Father. Even though He never sinned, He
willingly gave His life so that you and I could have eternal life.
He rose from the grave to show us that death had no power
over us. Just as He rose, we, too, will rise from the grave and
never see death again (John 8:51). After all that how can you
think that God does not care about you? God cares about
everything you are going through. He cares about the little
things that concern you just as much as the big things.

God promises to supply all your needs (Philippians 4:19). If
you need survival tools, ask God to supply them. If you need
peace, ask God to supply it. If you need anything at all, ask God

to supply it. He will supply every need you have. What kind of God would He be if His own children did not have the necessities of life? We serve a loving God who has the hairs on our head numbered. That is some kind of love.

# TASTE OF HIS GOODNESS

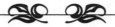

*Oh, taste and see that the Lord is good; blessed is the man who trusteth in Him.*

—Psalms 34:8

You can read testimony after testimony of God's miraculous deliverance and blessings on others, but until you experience Him for yourself, you will never really know. God is so good; there are no words that can adequately describe His goodness. Anyone who trusts in Him is blessed. They will be so blessed they will not lack any good thing (Psalms 34:10).

Remember how it was when your mom first told you that apples or some other fruit tasted good. You were not sure, but because she said it and she enjoyed it, you tried it yourself. When you took the first bite of that juicy fruit, it brought a smile to your face and your taste buds were happy. If you had not tried it for yourself, you would have never known how good it was. Well, it is the same way with Jesus. Not only is Jesus good, but having a relationship with the Lord is the best thing you could ever do. You can hear about how wonderful He is until the east meets the west, but unless you step out and give Him a try for yourself, you will never really know.

When we trust and rely upon God, we will experience His goodness. Give Jesus your heart. Try Him for yourself. Trust that He will not let you down. For the heart that is really seeking to know Him, He will go above and beyond to show Himself in a mighty way. He desires fellowship with you. He loves you and wants you to fall in love with Him. Let the Lord court you and be your best friend. You will never find another as sweet and good as our Lord.

# HOLD YOUR HEAD HIGH

*Take my yoke upon you, and learn of me; for I am meek and lowly in heart: and ye shall find rest unto your souls. For my yoke is easy, and my burden is light.*

—Matthew 11:29, 30

God has a rest for His people. He has given His Son, not only for our salvation, but so that we can have and enjoy life. It is impossible to enjoy life when we are burdened down with problems and issues that grieve us. Yes, there will always be problems in this world but they do not have to become burdens to us.

Jesus tells us to take His yoke upon us and learn of Him. He is a loving Savior who wants the very best for each of us. He has chosen to take on all our problems so that we do not have to be concerned about them. We can literally throw them on Him and let Him handle them. "Casting all your care upon Him; for He careth for you" (1 Peter 5:7).

Trying to handle all of life's problems in your own strength is like having a heavy yoke around your neck. Every day, it weighs you down more and more. When you try to hold your head up, your strength only lasts for a minute and then the weight of the yoke pulls you down again. Well, give that heavy yoke to Jesus today. Yokes can be many things including bills, marriage problems, children, a job or lack thereof, health problems, etc. Take the yoke off your neck and give it to the Lord. Then put on His yoke of peace, joy, mercy and grace and hold your head up high. For His yoke is easy and His burden is light.

# LET GOD TAKE CARE OF YOU

*Therefore I say unto you, take no thought for your life, what ye
shall eat, or what ye shall drink; nor yet for your body, what ye shall
put on. Is not the life more than meat, and the body than raiment?*
—Matthew 6:25

When Jesus says, "take no thought," what exactly does that
mean? I believe it means just what it says—that we are not even
supposed to think about our needs being met, much less worry
about them. If you take no thought, then you do not even waste
time thinking about such things.

We spend enormous amounts of time dwelling on ourselves
and our needs. God knows we have basic survival needs that
must be met and other needs, as well. What good would it be
to have an all-powerful and Almighty God as our Father and
He were unable to take care of our needs? How much work
could we do for the Kingdom if we had to figure out how to
survive on our own from day to day? Not much. You see God
wants to take care of us so that we can take care of our work
for Him.

If you are fretting about whether your needs will be met, stop
right now. God knows what you need. If you get out of the way,
He just might be able to take care of it, even permanently, so
you never have to think about it again. God does not want His
children to be naked, hungry or homeless. He has a vested
interest in your well-being. How can you show anybody God's
goodness if you do not have the necessities of life? God knows
quite well that you cannot. Therefore, trust God to take care
of you and stop worrying about it.

# JESUS IS YOUR FRIEND

*Henceforth I call you not servants; for the servant knoweth not what his Lord doeth: but I have called you friends; for all things that I have heard of my Father I have made known unto you.*

—John 15:15

*J*esus calls us His friends. What a blessing it is to have a friend like Jesus. He is a friend who sticks closer than a brother. He is a friend who is always available, 24-7, when you call. He is a friend who never leaves you nor forsakes you. He is a friend who never holds a grudge or seeks revenge. He is my best friend.

You have a wonderful friend in Jesus. He has given you His example and His Word so that you can have a victorious life. He even died for you so that you could have eternal life. "Greater love hath no man than this, that a man lay down his life for his friends" (John 15:13). Jesus is reaching out to you with out-stretched arms, always ready to love you and care for you.

Get to know your friend Jesus today. Spend some quality time with Him and fellowship with Him. He is truly wonderful. He will share everything with you. There is nothing He will not reveal to you—if you ask. Everything the Father gave Him, He freely gives to you because you are His friend. All He wants is for you to spend some time with Him and have a personal, intimate relationship with Him. Is that too much to ask from someone who gave His life for you?

I am truly honored that God calls me friend. Who am I that Almighty God would want to hang out with me? Yet, he does. And He wants to hang out with you, too.

# YOU BELONG TO GOD

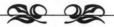

*All that the Father giveth me shall come to me; and him that cometh to me I will in no wise cast out.*

—John 6:37

If only we could love each other the way Jesus loves us. His love is the real deal. He takes us just the way we are, no questions asked and gives us eternal life in Him. What an awesome God we serve. I want you to think about that today as you pray. He was beaten, tortured, maimed, ridiculed, stabbed and crucified so that you could be redeemed back to God.

You may have gone back to your old ways or gotten out of fellowship with God. You may be mad at God for something that didn't go the way you wanted it to. Even still, Jesus loves you. He will never, ever forsake you or turn His back on you. All you have to do is repent and go back. His arms are always open wide.

God the Father has given you to Jesus. He chose you from the foundation of the world. You had absolutely nothing to do with your salvation. Jesus did it all and paid it all. When you answered His call and made Him Lord of your life, you were sealed forever. Even if you have messed up, God will not cast you out. You can never lose your salvation, no matter what you have done. Even if you are mad at God, He will not kick you out of the family. He loves you and is patiently waiting for you to come back to Him.

# MAKE IT PERSONAL

*As I was with Moses, so I will be with thee.*

—Joshua 3:7

The people that we read about in the Bible are real people who lived and breathed just like you and I. We sometimes forget that they went through many of the same trials and tribulations that we go through. We even think sometimes that they are made-up characters, but they are not.

Insert your name into the following sentence. "As I was with Moses, so I will be with (your name)." Just as God used Moses to part the Red Sea and bring forth water from a rock, He will use you to make a way out of no way and bring forth miracles. He will even do more than He did with Moses because we have the power of the Holy Spirit in us.

Make the promise of God personal in your own life. Take a pen and write in your name wherever you see a promise in the Bible. Then say it out loud so you hear it in your own ears and in your spirit. Believe it and receive it for yourself. All the promises of God are for you. They are still just as real as they were thousands of years ago. God never changes. His Word never changes, and it will not return void but will accomplish what God pleases (Isaiah 55:11).

# LOVE MAKES THE WORLD GO ROUND

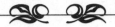

*Whosoever believeth that Jesus is the Christ is born of God: and every one that loveth Him that begat loveth him also that is begotten of Him.*

—1 John 5:1

How can you say you love God whom you have not seen and hate your brother who you see every day? God made each of us. He created us fearfully and wonderfully (Psalms 139:14). So when you really think about it, if you hate another person, you are hating God's creation; and if they are born-again, you might as well say that you are hating God because God lives in them.

Scripture says, "A new commandment I give unto you, that you love one another; as I have loved you, that ye also love one another" (John 13:34). When we love each other, it also says to the world that we are the children of God. "By this shall all men know that you are my disciples, if you have love one to another" (John 13:35).

It is imperative that we, as Christians, walk in love. We have to be the example for the world to see and follow. It will take a conscious effort for each of us to do this because as soon as we start, Satan will try to make sure it doesn't last.

Be prepared for people to come into your life and test your love. But hold fast, it is only a test. You can walk in love if you set your mind and heart to do it. Just remember, Jesus said, "This is my commandment, that ye love one another, as I have loved you" (John 15:12). No ifs, ands, or buts about it; we must love as Jesus loves.

# WHAT KIND OF LOVE IS THIS?

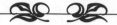

*Blessed be God, which hath not turned away my prayer, nor His mercy from me.*

—Psalms 66:20

I thank God today that He does not see me as a sinner any longer. I thank God today for His Son, Jesus, who chose to die for my sins, giving me the opportunity to choose Him as my Savior. I thank God today that He sees me as righteous even though I do not always walk and talk righteously. I thank God today that He hears my prayers and does not ever turn away from my voice. I thank God today that He has new mercy for me each morning. I thank God for being the wonderful, loving, merciful, gracious, kind and holy God that He is.

When I think about the kind of love and mercy God has for me, it boggles my mind. Just knowing how short I have come of the glory of God today, I wonder what kind of God is this, who never runs out of forgiveness, never gives up on me, and never stops pouring out His mercy and grace. He is an awesome God.

Don't ever stop praying. I don't care what you have done, God will hear your prayer, forgive your sins, and have mercy on you. Prayer is the key to forgiveness, restoration, and deliverance. Even when you do not know what or how to pray — pray anyway. Just sit at God's feet and say what is on your mind — that is prayer. Simply talking with God openly and honestly is prayer. Whether silently or out loud, on your knees or sitting in a chair, eyes closed or opened, crying or laughing, it is all prayer. Just do it and God will hear it. Not only that, He will answer, too.

# YOU'VE GOT A GREAT BENEFIT PACKAGE

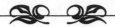

*What shall I render unto the Lord for all His benefits toward me?*
—Psalms 116:12

There are some great benefits to being born-again. Of course, the greatest benefit is eternal life in Heaven, but there are also many, many more. Here are just a few:

- Protection and safety
- Good health and healing
- Spiritual growth
- Financial prosperity
- Mental prosperity
- Having all your needs met
- Hearing from God
- Wisdom and revelation
- Comfort and peace
- Guidance and deliverance

Each and every day, you are loaded with these benefits and many more. You just need to receive them by faith.

We are so blessed to know the Lord. He has made life good for all who will receive it. That is why Jesus died, so that you could inherit God's promises. You can have a blessed life. You can enjoy your life. Isn't that something?

Really take a look at your benefit package with Jesus. You're covered in every area. There are no deductibles to pay, no fees and no penalties. You have full coverage. No company or insurance plan is more extensive than what Jesus offers. Sign up today. Oh, by the way—the cost…free.

# REAL LOVE REQUIRES ACTION

*The Lord thy God, He is God, the faithful God, which keepeth covenant and mercy with them that love Him and keep His commandments to a thousand generations.*

—Deuteronomy 7:9

𝒟o you really love the Lord? If you really love Him, then you will keep His commandments (John 14:21). That is how God judges your love for Him. Not by showing up at church on Sunday, not by putting large sums of money in the offering plate, not by doing a lot of charitable works, but by obeying His commands. Private actions speak louder than spoken words.

What good is it to go to church on Sunday, and curse out your neighbor on Monday? God commands us to love our neighbor as ourselves (Matthew 19:19). What good is it to give everything you have and not care about other people? It will profit you nothing (1 Corinthians 13:2). God commands that we love one another (John 13:34). What good is it to give to the poor and serve in ministry when you are committing adultery or stealing from your company? Are you loving the Lord when you disobey Him? Do you feel good about yourself when you know better? Real joy comes from having a clean conscience. When you are out of fellowship with God, inner joy and peace are missing.

Let us examine ourselves in the area of obedience and love. "If a man says, I love God, and hateth his brother, he is a liar: for he that loveth not his brother whom he hath seen, how can he love God whom he hath not seen?" (1 John 4:20). We need to love God for real. We need to spend quality time with Him so that we can experience His love for us. Then we can begin to share that love with others. All of God's commandments involve love—love for God, love for His Word, love for each other, even love for our enemies (Matthew 5:44). That is what sets us apart from the world and opens the door of God's wonderful blessings in our lives.

# DO YOU REALLY MEAN IT?

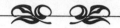

*As the Father hath loved me, so have I loved you: continue ye in my love.*

—John 15:9

*L*ove is a word that has somehow lost its meaning. It is thrown around so casually that the true meaning has grown cold. Real love is an awesome thing. The Bible says that God is love (1 John 4:8). Therefore, if God is love, then when we give love, we are giving God.

God takes love very seriously and so should we. "For God so loved the world, that He gave His only begotten Son" (John 3:16). Now that is some kind of love. We are to love everybody, even our enemies. Think about this—you were once God's enemy before you were saved. "But God commended His love toward us, in that, while we were yet sinners, Christ died for us" (Romans 5:8). One thing about God, He will never ask you to do something He has not already done.

Real love will cost you something. It is not flighty—here one day, gone the next. "Charity (love) suffereth long, and is kind; love envieth not; love vaunteth not itself, is not puffed up, doth not behave itself unseemly, seeketh not her own, is not easily provoked, thinketh no evil, rejoiceth not in iniquity, but rejoiceth in truth; beareth all things, believeth all things, hopeth all things, endureth all things. Love never faileth" (1 Corinthians 13:4-8).

The next time you say those beautiful words "I love you", think about love the way God does. Because of love, God gave

His life. Are you willing to give yours for the person you say you love? Are you giving people God when you give them love? Do you love those who mistreat you and hurt you and pray for them? Remember, real love costs something—but it is well worth the price.

# Spiritual Growth

# YOU HAVE GOODNESS AND MERCY

*Surely goodness and mercy shall follow me all the days of my life; and I will dwell in the house of the Lord for ever.*

—Psalms 23:6

*N*o matter where you go today, you will have two spiritual forces going with you: goodness and mercy. They are constant companions to all of God's children. God's goodness and mercy are eternal. They will last all the days of your earthly life and for eternity after. I want you to let this truth really sink into your spirit. When you really know you have the forces of God with you, you walk a little differently. You have a confidence that may baffle others around you, but you know where it comes from.

A trick of the enemy is to keep you ignorant of the truth. Why? "And ye shall know the truth, and the truth shall make you free" (John 8:32). The enemy does not want you to be free. He wants you to stay trapped in bondage. Ignorance of the truth of God's Word gives the enemy room to fill our minds with lies and deceit. These lies become so ingrained in our souls that when truth is presented to us, many times we reject it.

Good is supposed to happen to you. You are surrounded by goodness and you have goodness in you. Expect good. Believe that something good is going to happen today.

We receive new mercy every day (Lamentations 3:23). That is the truth. Believe it. God will give you mercy. He is giving you mercy right now. You have a merciful Savior who wants to see you make it. He is good and merciful.

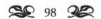

98

I implore you to be on a quest for truth—God's truth—about who He is, who you are in Him, and what the future holds. It's all there in the Book. You must be diligent. "For he that cometh to God must believe that He is, and that He is a rewarder of them that diligently seek Him" (Hebrews 11:6b). Your reward will be great. You will know the truth and the truth will make you free—indeed!

# FEAR NOT

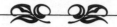

*I sought the Lord, and He heard me, and delivered me from all my fears.*

—Psalms 34:4

We have all experienced fear—fear of the future, fear of failure, fear of the dark and fear of death. Then there are phobias, including fear of flying, fear of heights and fear of germs. The Bible teaches us that "God has not given us the spirit of fear; but of power, and of love, and of a sound mind" (2 Timothy 1:7). So how do we combat the spirit of fear? By exercising faith in God.

Faith is the opposite of fear. When we walk by faith, we annul fear. Faith says "my future is in God's hand, and He has a good plan for me. There is no failure in God. I am a child of light and I shall not fear what man can do to me. My times are in God's hand, and He knows my beginning from my ending." Faith says, "I can," while fear says, "I can't."

Fear also opens the door for the enemy, Satan, to come in and bring your fears to pass. You must close the door with the Word. For example, if you begin to think that you will not make it and nothing good is going to happen to you, tell yourself, "Surely goodness and mercy shall follow me all the days of my life: and I will dwell in the house of the Lord for ever"(Psalms 23:6), or "Eye hath not seen, nor ear heard, neither have entered into the heart of man, the things which God hath prepared for them that love Him" (1 Corinthians 2:9). If the enemy tells you that you're sick and going to die, you tell him,

"By His stripes, I am healed!" (Isaiah 53:5; 1 Peter 2:24) "And the Lord will take away from me all sickness" (Deuteronomy 7:15). You must use God's Word against the enemy and you must believe the Word of God that you speak. It will cause Satan to flee every time.

The next time you are attacked by fear remember that it is coming from the enemy. Rebuke him, stand on God's Word. That is why you must study and face your fears. That is the only way to conquer the fear—just do it. God is by your side. Say to yourself, "I can do all things through Christ, who strengthens me!" (Philippians 4:13) and break the bondage of fear in your life.

# NO TIME FOR SELF-PITY

*And the Lord turned the captivity of Job, when he prayed for his friends; also the Lord gave Job twice as much as he had before.*
—Job 42:10

*O*ne of the best cures for self-pity is to think about the problems of others. When I read the book of Job, I realize that my tragedies and suffering were little in comparison to his. Remember, Job lost everything—his wealth, all seven of his children, his health—and even his wife turned against him. Now that's suffering. You may not know of anyone personally who has endured this kind of trial, but remember that there is always someone who is worse off than you.

Job knew that God was good and that God was his only hope. We would do well to learn from Job, because in the end, God not only restored all that Job lost, He doubled his blessings. And do you know when God blessed him? When Job took his mind off himself and prayed for his friends.

The greatest thing you can do for God is to trust Him with your problems by casting the care on Him and becoming a blessing to someone else, even while you are going through difficulties. Not only will it take your mind off yourself, it will show someone else the goodness of God through your actions.

The Christmas after my son died, I took the money I would have used to buy gifts for him and bought clothes and toys for two small children who did not have much. It gave me so much joy to be able to bless someone else, even though I was hurting. God has given me so much back in return, that space and time will not allow me to tell it all.

*Norma DeShields Brown*

Try it for yourself. Be a blessing to another person. It does not have to involve money. You can spend a little time with an elderly person, read a story to a young child, visit someone in the hospital, or call up a relative or friend you have not spoken to in a long time. Just follow the leading of the Spirit of God and watch how God will bless you in return.

# GET WISDOM

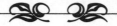

*Wisdom is the principal thing; therefore, get wisdom, and with all thy getting, get understanding.*

—Proverbs 4:7

*G*od asked King Solomon, "What shall I give thee?" You know what his reply was—to have "an understanding heart to judge thy people, that I may discern between good and bad" (1 Kings 3:9). Solomon wanted to have a spirit of discernment. He knew that godly wisdom and discernment would ensure his success as king.

That should be our desire, as well. If we have the mind of Christ and can hear from God when we need answers to life's problems, we will have everything we need to be successful and happy. Godly wisdom gives us the tools to get wealth, have a happy marriage, raise godly children, maintain good health, and receive all the desires of our hearts.

The Bible says, "If any of you lack wisdom, let him ask of God, that giveth to all men liberally and upbraideth not; and it shall be given him" (James 1:5). It also says, "Ye have not, because ye ask not" (James 4:2). Ask God to give you wisdom and discernment. Ask Him to give you understanding in areas where you need it. God wants you to succeed. He needs you to succeed so unbelievers will see you living a successful and prosperous life and will want to know your secret. Then you can glorify God and lead them to Christ.

Wisdom is the principal thing that we need to live in victory here on earth. The world will tell you that money, or beauty, or some other natural thing is most important. We know that without wisdom, money will cause more problems than it will solve, and it also won't last very long. The world's standard of beauty will fade with age, and then what?

God already has a plan for your success and happiness. All you have to do is ask for it. He may give it to you one step at a time, but trust Him and enjoy the ride. Get your priorities in line with God's and seek Him first. He will give you all the answers you will need for every situation you will face.

# READ THE INSTRUCTION MANUAL

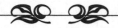

*Take fast hold of instruction; let her not go. Keep her; for she is thy life.*

—Proverbs 4:13

The Word of God is our instruction manual for life. It gives us the recipe for joy, peace, prosperity and salvation. All we have to do is read it, get understanding, and do it. It's no different than buying a new microwave oven and taking out the instruction booklet to see how to operate it. God has given us a proven instruction manual on how to live and enjoy life.

Are you dissatisfied with circumstances in your life? Do you feel that things could be better, if only you knew what to do? I'll be honest with you, I've felt that way and I'm sure everybody has at one time or another. God has given us the answers we are looking for, but we must take the time to get the instruction manual and find them out (2 Timothy 3:16, 17). Let's change that today. Seek the One who has all the answers. Go to the Source. Surely, He knows how to fix our problems.

My personal formula is this: (1) pray; (2) read and study God's Word; and (3) believe. Pray that God will reveal to you His plan and His answers for your life. Develop a personal and intimate relationship with Him. Go to Him in prayer about everything.

Take your Bible off the coffee table and read it. Ask God to show you the answer in His Word that applies to your situation. Seek His wisdom, and by all means use the concordance. Look up topics and words that fit your particular problem or situation. The Bible is an unlimited source of guidance and instruction for us. The book of Proverbs literally tells us what to do, what not to do, and how to live.

Finally, believe what God's Word says. It's one thing to read it and say, "That sounds nice." It's another to read it and say, I receive that as truth. I believe in my heart what God's Word says over my situation. This may not be easily done at first. But if you keep reading—sometimes the same scripture over and over, saying it out loud, and meditating on it—you will soon get it embedded in your heart and your belief and faith in God will change your situation and solve your problems.

I know that may sound too good to be true, but don't knock it until you try it. What do you have to lose? You have been trying to fix the problem but it's still there, or it has come back again. This time go to the instruction manual, the Holy Bible, and read what the Manufacturer has to say. I guarantee He'll fix it once and for all.

# WHO CAN BE A VIRTUOUS WOMAN?

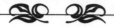

*She stretcheth out her hand to the poor; yea, she reacheth forth her hands to the needy.*

—Proverbs 31:20

Most of you have heard of the virtuous woman. She is truly a superwoman to the tenth degree. You may have even read Proverbs 31 and thought, "How can I possibly be like her?" I've asked myself the same question. The key, I believe, is found in verses 30 and 31: "Charm can be deceptive and beauty doesn't last, but a woman who fears, and reverences God shall be greatly praised. Praise her for the many fine things she does. These good deeds of hers shall bring her honor and recognition from even the leaders of the nations." If we want to be like the woman portrayed in this chapter, whether we are male or female, we must first fear and reverence God. In addition, we should also do good deeds, such as helping the poor and needy.

God said that when we give, it shall be returned back to us in good measure, pressed down, shaken together, and running over (Luke 6:38). When we help those who are less fortunate than we are, we are doing what Jesus taught us to do—loving one another (John 15:17). We must not get so caught up in our problems or our success and forget that there are hurting people in the world who need love. Something as small as smiling or saying hello can brighten someone's day.

When we have Jesus living on the inside of us, we cannot help but to love people. Jesus loved people—all people, even people that society tossed aside. Extending compassion and mercy is natural for those who have received compassion and mercy from God. When we help others and become a blessing, we are blessed all the more by our heavenly Father. God blesses us so that we can be a blessing to someone else.

I encourage you to be a blessing to someone today. Help an organization that is reaching out to those less fortunate either with your financial support, time, or prayer. Give away some of those old clothes in your closet that are just taking up space. Call a friend who has been on your mind. Pray for our nation and our leaders. There are so many needs in our world, you can easily find someone to bless. I guarantee you that you won't have time to dwell on yourself when you are busy helping others. Soon you will be reaping the harvest of all you have sown; and just like the virtuous woman, you will receive honor and recognition.

# ABIDE IN THE VINE

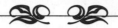

*I am the vine, ye are the branches. He that abideth in me, and I in him, the same bringeth forth much fruit; for without me ye can do nothing.*

—John 15:5

Jesus said plainly, "for without me you can do nothing." That tells me that anything I undertake in life must be rooted in Christ. I need Him in order to succeed; I can do nothing apart from Him. Well, then, why do I keep coming up with my own plans and trying to make them work myself? Why am I not surprised when it all blows up in my face? Why do I keep making the same mistakes over and over? Because I am not following the manual!

God knows how to do what we have trouble doing. He has all the answers to every question. We do not have to be stressed out every day. We can abide in Christ. Well, you may ask, "What does that mean?" To "abide" means to dwell in, remain in, or settle in. Start by learning about Him. Reading the Bible is the best way to learn of Him. When you read the Bible you are actually reading the Word of God. John 1:1 says, "In the beginning was the Word and the Word was with God, and the *Word was God*." God is His Word. Abiding in Him means your will succumbs to His will. You choose to do what He says do, and not what your flesh wants to do. You allow God to rule and reign in your everyday life.

There is no limit to what you can do in Christ. All things are possible with God (Matthew 19:26). Without Him you can do nothing. Even if you manage to successfully complete your task on your own without consulting God, the Bible says, "Except the Lord build the house, they labour in vain that build it"(Psalms 127:1). In other words, you may be able to create your own plan, successfully implement it and get it to prosper, but it will all come to naught. If God is not in it, it will not last.

Get to know the Lord. Let Him be the one to order your steps. Give your life over to Him. Abide in His Word and seek Him in everything.

# WHAT'S ON YOUR MIND?

*Thou wilt keep him in perfect peace, whose mind is stayed on thee, because he trusteth in thee.*

—Isaiah 26:3

The Bible says we are to seek peace and pursue it (1 Peter 3:11). One of the ways to accomplish that is to keep our thoughts on God and His Word. Isaiah 26:3 tells us that God, not we ourselves, will keep us in peace when we keep our mind stayed on Him—when we trust God and not our circumstances.

It is really not hard for us to live a peaceful life. It requires renewing our minds, but we can actually believe God's Word and trust Him to always take care of us. If we would do that, we would never worry or be stressed out about the things going on in our world. The key word, however, is *if*. We have to make the decision to live in peace by seeking and pursuing it. Our manual for living—the Holy Bible—tells us plainly how to do this.

The questions you must ask yourself are: Do I really want to have peace in my life? Am I willing to step out in faith and believe God? If the answer to both of these questions is yes—and I hope it is—just do it. Take control of your thoughts minute by minute and retrain them to focus on and think about God's promises and ways. When negative or evil thoughts come into your mind, *stop* and tell yourself, "No that is a lie, God's Word says…" Even say it out loud if you have to. This is serious, so you may have to take radical measures to have peace. Again, you must know God's Word. Peace begins with knowing exactly what God has to say about everyday situations. I do not think studying and knowing the Word is too high a price to pay for inner peace. Do you?

Peace of mind is a precious commodity in this day and age. There is so much pressure and stress that keeps us in turmoil. For some of us, it seems like peace is only a fantasy, something that really is impossible to have. You can have peace, if you really want it. The choice is yours. It will take some work and effort, but you can attain and keep inner peace—the kind of peace that is not contingent upon everything being just the way you want. You can have peace that comes from within your spirit, knowing God is in control.

Keep your mind on the things of God. Not only will it bring you peace, you will have unspeakable joy to go along with it. Life can be worth living, when we give it to God.

# DON'T WAIT TO REFUEL YOUR SPIRITUAL TANK

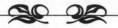

*Trust ye in the Lord for ever; for in the Lord Jehovah is everlasting strength.*

—Isaiah 26:4

How often do you say the words "I am so tired" or "I'm just worn-out"? Most people say it so often they would not be able to count the number of times, even if their lives depended on it. Sometimes, we really are tired and worn-out. Depression, grief, sadness, and anger require an enormous amount of our energy. Have you noticed that after a good crying spell, you feel tired? It is at those times that we become more vulnerable to the wiles of the devil. He likes to attack when we are weak and unprepared to fight him off. It is a strategy that has given him many victories, but it does not have to be that way.

When we get weak or tired, we have One inside of us to strengthen and help us—the Holy Spirit. The Holy Spirit is the Strengthener. As the Spirit of God, He knows when our strength has run out. The Holy Spirit lives inside every born-again believer. He is there to provide all the help we need, when we need it, no matter what it is—strength, comfort, wisdom, peace, discernment, whatever. The Holy Spirit wants to be used. He wants to help you. Let Him.

I have often thought about how children, trying to grow up faster than they should, will refuse help from their parents. Many parents will sit back and watch the child mess up over and over until he or she finally gives up and asks for help. It is much the same way with God. He is always right there to help us, but we struggle and try to do it ourselves. We fail or wear ourselves out and refuse to ask God for help. All the while, God waits patiently until we give up and finally turn to Him for help. He sends the help we need, but just like little children, we keep trying to do things ourselves first.

Let's grow up. God is ready and willing to help us. Why waste precious time trying to handle your problems, your family, and your own life, only to mess up and have to call on God to fix it anyway. Let's make a strong effort to call on God in the beginning. Then we will not have to tire ourselves out trying to do all of the things the world demands that we do, in our own strength.

God never gets tired. He never goes to sleep. He is always available, anytime, anyplace. He lives right inside of your spirit, ready whenever you call. Be smart and call often. Let Him strengthen you, so you can run the race that is set before you.

# PRUNING IS ESSENTIAL

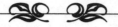

*Beloved, now are we the children of God, and it doth not appear what we shall be; but we know that, when He shall appear, we shall be like Him; for we shall see Him as He is.*

—1 John 3:2

You are being transformed into the image of Christ day by day. Where you are today is not where you will be. Time has a great way of allowing us to heal and grow into the image of Christ.

Do not despise where you are right now. God has you exactly where you need to be. He is in control of your development. I know there are times when we get frustrated with our spiritual growth. We feel that we should be further along in some particular area. Pray about the area you feel you are behind in. Turn it over to God and let Him guide you through at His pace. He is the only one who knows exactly how to cause us to grow in the right way and at just the right time. God is never late, and He will never fail.

Sometimes we are being pruned and purged of character and behaviors that are not like God. This may take some time. We have spent years developing these attitudes and behaviors, so don't expect them to disappear overnight. Pruning is not a pleasant experience. If plants could talk, I am sure they would tell us that getting their branches cut and leaves trimmed is uncomfortable. Pruning is also uncomfortable for us. That is why God must take His time. He knows just where to cut and how much to trim.

I have often wanted God to speed up the pruning process in my life. But I've found that God is going to take His perfect time. While we are being pruned, we will develop patience. God knows how to make your pruning the most profitable for you. I thank Him for it because when we finally see Him, it will truly be well worth any work, pain, or suffering we have experienced. God's Word tells us, "For our light affliction, which is but for a moment, worketh for us a far more exceeding and eternal weight of glory" (2 Corinthians 4:17).

# WHAT'S IN YOUR HEAVENLY ACCOUNT?

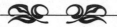

*But my God shall supply all your need according to His riches in glory by Christ Jesus.*

—Philippians 4:19

The Bible tells us that Christ is the Creator of all things that are in Heaven and that are in the earth (Colossians 1:16). Everything belongs to Him. So when we have a need in our lives, wouldn't it make good sense to go to the One who has what we need?

Paul wrote to the Philippians so they would not worry about their daily needs. They had given financially to help take care of him. He let them know that their gifts were fruit that abounded to their account (Philippians 4:17). God wants us to support the work of the ministry so fruit can abound to our account. Then when we have a need, we can call on God to supply it from our own heavenly account. "But lay up for yourselves treasures in heaven, where neither moth nor rust doth corrupt, and where thieves do not break through nor steal" (Matthew 6:20). Since you cannot mail a check to Heaven addressed to Jesus, you lay up your heavenly treasure by paying your tithes, ten per cent of your income and offerings to your church. Also by giving offerings to other ministries and godly charities, helping the poor by donating food, clothing, money, or time, and serving in ministry.

God will supply your needs even when you have not given. He takes care of us because He loves us. But we can get into the realm of having more than enough when we start to operate in God's laws and principles. We can have our needs met and also be able to meet the needs of others when we give as God directs us to.

Get into the "more than enough" status today. Plant your seed, giving into good soil that will produce a large harvest. Stop worrying about your needs and turn them over to God. He will supply them. Stand on His Word. Jesus asked in Matthew 6:27, "Which of you by taking thought can add one cubit unto his stature?" So quit worrying. Let God take care of you as you take care of God's kingdom here on earth.

# DEVELOP YOUR FAITH

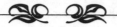

*So then faith cometh by hearing, and hearing by the word of God.*
—Romans 10:17

If you are like me, there have been times that you wished you had someone else's faith. It seemed that the preachers and television evangelists had a level of faith that I could never reach. What I failed to realize was that God is no respecter of person and that my faith is increased the more I read, speak, and hear God's Word.

Our faith is increasingly developed as we renew our minds with the Word. Romans 12:2 says, "And be not conformed to this world, but be ye transformed by the renewing of your mind, that ye may prove what is that good, and acceptable, and perfect, will of God." Our minds have to be renewed. The only way to do that is with the Word of the living God. We literally must become "brainwashed."

As you begin to read, hear and speak the Word more and more, your faith will begin to increase. As you test the Word and see God work for yourself, the level of your faith will automatically rise. You will stop doubting and start believing. You will start to walk by faith and not by sight. It is a gradual process that will take some time to develop. So be patient with yourself. When you see other people who have a deeper and stronger faith than yours, just know they have had more experience with God and their faith has been developed to that level. You will get there; just keep on believing and trusting God.

# BE THANKFUL

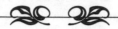

*And ye shall eat in plenty, and be satisfied, and praise the name of the Lord your God, that hath dealt wondrously with you; and my people shall never be ashamed.*

—Joel 2:26

When God blesses us are we truly grateful and thankful? Come on now, be real. Sometimes we take for granted the blessings God gives to us every day. The scripture tells us that when God cares for us and makes sure we have plenty, we should praise the name of the Lord because He has dealt wondrously with us.

You know, there is always someone who is worse off than you. No matter how bad you think your life is, it could be worse. The fact that you have another opportunity to change and improve your life is worth praising God for. Thank Him that you have life; thank Him that you have food; thank Him that you have clothes to wear. We take these things for granted, but there are people who are hungry, some are naked, and many who did not wake up this morning. You have another shot at it. Many people would like to be in your shoes!

Be thankful even in the hard times. Don't be angry if you are going through a trial right now. Be thankful that God has given you this opportunity to grow. God has promised that you will not be put to shame.

Once I was fired from a job for no reason. Because of politics, my livelihood was stripped from me. However, I held my head up high, knowing I had all I needed in God. I knew that God would take care of me and would open another door for me, one that was better than the door that closed. God has not failed me, nor will He fail you. If you are experiencing hard times right now, consider those who are struggling through much more than you this very moment.

What do you have to thank God for? I am sure the list is long, so you might want to write it down on paper. It does your soul good to see for yourself just how good God is to you. Write down everything from having ten toes and fingers to your mansion on the hill. It is because of God's grace that we have anything at all, and everything we have belongs to God. Bless His holy name for all He has done and will do for you.

# FEAR NO MAN

*The Lord is my light and my salvation; whom shall I fear? The Lord is the strength of my life; of whom shall I be afraid?*
—Psalms 27:1

God has said, "No weapon that is formed against thee shall prosper" (Isaiah 54:17). Now, it does not say that there will be no weapons formed against you. There will be weapons, I can guarantee that. However, they will be defeated, and you will win. They will not prosper. Therefore, you need not fear anything or anybody.

The enemy will try to use people to hurt us and destroy us. Very often, he uses the people who are closest to us. His attempts will not succeed if we stand firm in God's salvation. God has saved us, not just from Hell, but from anything that tries to kill, steal, or destroy us. That's why King David could say, "The Lord is my light and my salvation; whom shall I fear?" He realized that no one was more powerful than God. God was on his side, so he had the victory even before he could see it.

Yes, we will have battles and weapons formed against us. We may get weary of fighting, but God has said that He will be our strength. When we cannot seem to go any further, that is when we need to call on the Lord. He will step in where we are weak. Hallelujah!

You are not out there fighting the enemy by yourself. God is fighting with you, and He will get the victory and strengthen you. So hang in there. The battle is already won, but God wants you to have the spoils, too. Do not worry and do not be afraid. People cannot do any harm to you. They will just set you up to be blessed. If things get a little dark, don't fret; God is your light. If you get tired and weary, don't give up; let God be your strength. And when the battle is over, not only will you have defeated the enemy, but you will have blessings upon blessings to show for your courageous efforts in battle.

# WAIT

*Wait on the Lord; be of good courage, and He shall strengthen thine heart. Wait, I say, on the Lord.*

—Psalms 27:14

*O*ne of the hardest things for believers to do is to wait. However, it is a universal experience because we must wait in order to receive God's blessings and His best for us. Waiting is not easy to do. The enemy knows that, so he will try to get us to doubt God and become impatient. He hopes we will try to attain our desire by ourselves, apart from God, which usually ends in disaster. The irony is that we end up waiting longer when we interfere than if we had been still and just waited on God. "Except the Lord build the house, they labour in vain that build it" (Psalms 127:1a).

God does not always answer our prayers immediately. However, He does answer our prayers, even if the answer is "no" or "wait." These are not the answers we like to hear, but they are necessary when we are not ready to receive the answer or we are asking for something that is outside of God's will for us. God knows the right time to bring the answer to our prayers into our hands. So be patient. It's on the way. Trust God, believe and thank Him for it now. When God sees that we are really believing and not doubting, He will bring it to pass. Jesus said in Mark 11:22-23, "Have faith in God. For verily I say unto you, That whosoever shall say unto this mountain, Be thou removed, and be thou cast into the sea; and shall not doubt in his heart, but shall believe that those things which he saith shall come to pass; he shall have whatsoever he saith."

You will receive when you believe. Do not be tricked into doubt and unbelief. It is one of the enemy's greatest tools for stealing our blessings. God cannot send it if you are no longer believing for it, because you might think it came from another source other than God. He must get all the glory and honor because it is God who blesses you with all you possess.

While you are waiting on your answer from God, let God strengthen you with His Word. Rejoice and be glad because God did hear you, and He will come through for you. It's just a matter of His perfect timing. Continue to walk by faith and not by sight. Soon, you will receive all that you believe that God will do for you.

# PRAY FOR ONE ANOTHER

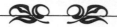

*Confess your faults one to another, and pray one for another, that ye may be healed. The effectual fervent prayer of a righteous man availeth much.*

—James 5:16

When you are suffering, one of the best things you can do to promote healing is to pray for and help someone else. It not only takes your mind off your own problems for a while, it also causes you to be a blessing, which in turn blesses you back. God is very wise in the way He has created us. In His system of operation, you get blessed when you are a blessing. When you give, then you receive. When you sow, then you reap. In His plan, you must first do and then you get. It causes you to forgo selfishness and self-centeredness and think about someone else.

Our natural tendency is to feel sorry for ourselves, keep our mind on our problems and have an attitude because we are having a bad day. God says that we should confess our faults to another brother or sister in Christ who will not judge us.

For example, we could say something like, "I am really having a bad day. I just want to scream and tear somebody's head off." Let them pray for you and you also pray for them because the prayers of the righteous will bring change.

The next time you are feeling down, mad or sorry for yourself, call up a friend and bless them, or go out and help somebody. Get your mind off yourself. You can't fix the problem anyway, or you would. Help someone else who might be feeling down, mad or sorry for themselves, and God will take care of you. When you take care of God's plans or His people, then God will take care of you.

# ARE YOU SUBMITTED?

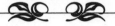

*Submit yourselves, therefore, to God. Resist the devil, and he will flee from you.*

—James 4:7

$\mathcal{M}$ost people only quote half of James 4:7. They are quick to say, "Resist the devil, and he will flee." However, the Scripture begins by saying, "Submit yourselves therefore to God." That condition is the key to the fulfillment of the entire Scripture. If we do not first submit to God, we will not have the power to resist the devil; and even if we did, it would be in our own strength and it would not last very long. The devil would keep on coming until he just wore us out.

Learn to give God first place in your life. Submit to His Word and make a conscious decision that you are going to live by it. Study it so that you know what it says and what you are to do. How do you submit yourself to God? By doing what the Word says. When you are living a submitted and obedient life, you can easily recognize and resist the devil, and you will have authority in the name of Jesus that will make the devil flee. It is as simple as that. The reason it is hard for us to submit is the flesh. It wants to run wild and out of control. So start getting that wild flesh of yours under control. Tell it *"No!"*

We all submit to someone—a boss, spouse, parent or pastor. Why not submit to God, who always has our best interest at heart. It just makes good sense.

# SORROW-FREE WEALTH

*The blessing of the Lord, it maketh rich, and He addeth no sorrow with it.*

—Proverbs 10:22

*R*eal wealth is not in the accumulation of cash and things. Real wealth is salvation, peace, joy and wisdom. Yes, God does want us to have financial abundance and the things we desire. However, there are many "cash rich" people who are miserable and unhappy. Money does not equal peace or joy. My prayer is that we would all be like King Solomon and ask for wisdom. When we have wisdom, we will know how to get money and know what to do with it. We will also know that spiritual growth is far more valuable than financial blessings alone. The Bible goes so far as to say that "Wisdom is the principal thing; therefore get wisdom" (Proverbs 4:7).

When we have financial abundance without wisdom, it can lead to our destruction and cause more problems than it solves. The Bible is full of stories about people who mismanaged money and wealth. When we seek spiritual wisdom first, then God will show us how to receive and manage money properly and be a blessing to others. Therefore, when God prospers us His way, we have wealth with no trouble added to it. We can walk in true prosperity knowing God will continue to prosper us as long as we are obedient to His commands and we use our resources to be a blessing to those in need and to promote the kingdom of God.

"But seek ye first the kingdom of God, and His righteous-

ness; and all these things shall be added unto you" (Matthew 6:33). Pray and ask God to give you wisdom so that you will be mature in the things of God and He can pour out His blessings on you in abundance. God wants you to prosper; He takes pleasure in your prosperity if you are His servant. Seek and serve the Lord with all your heart. He will gladly bless you and make you rich, and you will have no sorrow with it.

# PROSPERITY IS GOD'S #1 DESIRE FOR YOU

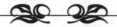

*Beloved, I wish above all things that thou mayest prosper and be in health, even as thy soul prospereth.*

—3 John 2

*F*or all of you who mistakenly thought that financial prosperity and good health were just nice things to wish for but you were not likely to have, 3 John 2 proves that is not true. God wishes above all things that you would prosper and be in good health just as He wants you to prosper in your soul. So clearly understand this: you are supposed to be prosperous in every area of your life—financially, physically, socially, spiritually and mentally. Talk about having it all! When you are truly prosperous, you do have it all.

We are supposed to be so blessed and prosperous that people will constantly ask us to share our secret to success. Everyone will want to know how we did it. That's our opportunity to share the Gospel and the truth that it is only because of God's grace that we prosper. Then we can lead them to our source — Jesus Christ. That is why God wants you to prosper so we can show Him off. "For the eyes of the Lord run to and fro throughout the whole earth, to shew Himself strong in the behalf of them whose heart is perfect toward Him" (2 Chronicles 16:9).

The first step to receiving your prosperity is knowing that God wants you to have it. Faith says you believe you have it even before you see it. If you are sick in your body, believe you are healed today. Start speaking healing out of your own mouth as though it already were so. Then get scriptures about healing and meditate on them. Speak them out loud so that you hear them. Faith comes by hearing. The same holds true with finances and spiritual growth. If you do not believe you can have it, you will not have it. "For as he thinketh in his heart, so is he" (Proverbs 23:7).

# KEEP HOPE ALIVE

*Now the God of hope fill you with all joy and peace in believing,*
*that ye may abound in hope, through the power of the Holy Ghost.*
—Romans 15:13

There is so much joy and peace in believing God. He is the God of hope! What would life be like without hope? Pretty bad, wouldn't you say? Yet, there are people all over the world that have no hope. Their lives are in such a rut that they think they will never escape. They cannot see a brighter tomorrow, so they feel deeply discouraged and think, "What's the use?"

But we have a God who gives us hope for a fabulous future. We know that we may not be where we want to be, but we are not where we used to be, and each day brings us more and more victory. Even when it seems like things are not so good, we know that all things are working together for our good (Romans 8:28) and in due season we shall reap if we faint not (Galatians 6:9). Keep on hoping, child of God, because faith is the substance of things hoped for (Hebrews 11:1). God operates based on our faith so call those things which are not, as though they were (Romans 4:17).

What are your hopes and dreams today? Dream big! You have a big God, who is not limited at all. Do you dream to have your own business? A new or first home? A new car, boat or plane? A local or worldwide ministry? A family? Whatever your hope or desire, God is able to do it. He is the God of your hopes and dreams. As long as you are plugged in to the power source, the Holy Spirit, there is nothing you and God cannot do.

"Now unto Him that is able to do exceeding abundantly above all that we ask or think, according to the power that worketh in us" (Ephesians 3:20). God can only do exceeding abundantly above what we ask or think according to the amount of power that is working in us. Are you plugged in? If not, get plugged in by reading the Word, renewing your mind with the Word, and obeying the Word. Once you have gotten plugged in, keep yourself charged up with praise, worship and fellowship. If you are filled with the Holy Spirit you have the power…so get powered up! God is waiting to pour out His exceeding grace on you.

# RENEW YOUR STRENGTH

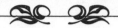

*But they that wait upon the Lord shall renew their strength; they shall mount up with wings as eagles; they shall run, and not be weary; and they shall walk, and not faint.*

—Isaiah 40:31

*O*ur human nature wants to get what we want, when we want it. However, God's timing is perfect, and He is not moved by our impatience. We must learn to wait on the Lord if we are going to have real victory in our lives. He does not always move in our timing, yet He is always on time.

Waiting is not easy, and therefore, it takes maturity on our part. Babies never want to wait; they do not understand patience. When we begin our walk with God, we are spiritual babies. We have to renew our minds so that the way we think lines up with God's way of thinking.

When we make our desires and petitions to God in prayer, immediately God goes to work. It may take a while for the manifestation of God's answers to come to pass. However, God promises they will come to pass; He just does not say when. We know that Satan is going to try and steal our blessing before it ever reaches us. That is why we must wait patiently on the Lord, because our faith and determination to receive from God gives the angels power to bring the blessings and allows God to do the work that needs to be done in us.

Do not faint or get weary. That is the very thing that will keep you from receiving what you are believing God for. Wait on God, knowing that He is working behind the scenes on your behalf. He sees the big picture, and you see only in part. Trust that He knows exactly what He is doing, and He will not be a second late. Renew your strength today by standing on the promises of God concerning your desire and wait on the Lord. He will come through for you. In the meantime, get your strength renewed and mount up like an eagle soaring high above the wickedness of this world.

# HIT THE POWER SWITCH

*He that spared not His own Son, but delivered Him up for us all,
how shall He not with Him also freely give us all things?*

—Romans 8:32

You have been praying and believing God for a specific blessing in your life. You've been patiently waiting for the manifestation of it, yet it has not come. You have times of doubt when you think God is not going to come through, and you even wonder if He knows who you are. Those are normal thoughts, and we've all had them at one time or another. But read Romans 8:32 again and let it get into your spirit. Read it over and over until you get the revelation that God wants you to have.

God not only knows you, He made you. And not only that, He gave His only begotten Son for you (John 3:16). If He would do that for you, what makes you doubt that He will give you what you ask for? He will give you more than what you ask for! The Bible says, "Now unto Him who is able to do exceeding abundantly above all that we ask or think, according to the power that worketh in us" (Ephesians 3:20). So that tells you that He will do more than what you ask, but it is according to the power that is at work in you.

Is your power source low? The Holy Spirit is the power that operates in all who are born again. However, you have to submit to His authority and leading. He is a gentleman and will not go any further than you give Him permission. Doubt will kill the power fast. You must be committed to believing God's Word, no matter what.

God wants to bless you, but if you do not really believe He can or will then you are cutting off the power that will bring the blessing to pass. It's up to you, so let the power flow.

# IT'S TIME TO GROW UP

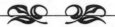

*For the word of God is quick and powerful, and sharper than any two-edged sword, piercing even to the dividing asunder of soul and spirit, and of the joints and marrow, and is a discerner of the thoughts and intents of the heart.*

—Hebrews 4:12

*L*et me ask you a question. Do you really want to have the abundant life Jesus died for you to have? If you really do, it is going to cost you something. You are going to have to grow up spiritually and die to self. I know that is not what you wanted to hear. You would probably prefer to be reminded about God's love and told how much He was going to bless you today. Well, He does love you and He will bless you. However, there comes a time when we have to go a little deeper than that. We have to grow up.

Our flesh-body, and our soul-mind, will and emotions often cause our problems. The spirit wants to do the will of God, but the flesh wants to do what it feels like doing. The only way we are going to give the spirit, which is outnumbered two to one, the upper hand is by renewing our minds with the Word of God. The Word tells us that "All scripture is given by inspiration of God, and is profitable for doctrine, for reproof, for correction, for instruction in righteousness, that the man of God may be perfect, thoroughly furnished unto all good works" (2 Timothy 3:16-17). Everything in the Bible is direct instruction from God to change us and grow us up spiritually.

The Word of God should agitate you sometimes. Part of its purpose is to divide your soul from your spirit, so that the spirit will be in control. The cutting or dividing asunder should not be comfortable. However, it is necessary in order for you to renew your mind. The Word of God should make you see yourself and desire to change. The Word of God is spiritual food. It gives nourishment to your spirit and causes you to grow. We all start out as babes needing milk. But after a while we grow to a point where we can start chewing on some stronger meat and vegetables.

God is not going to give power, money and success to an immature baby because he or she will not know how to handle it. So if you really want to have abundant life, let the Word of God work on you daily to divide your soul and spirit. Then when you are fully grown, you will have abundant life and be willing and able to do good works, which glorify God.

# BEEN THERE, DONE THAT

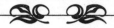

*As for God, His way is perfect; the word of the Lord is tried; He is
a buckler to all those that trust in Him.*

—Psalms 18:30

*W*e often view God's way of doing things as strange and
unusual. Granted, God's ways are not like the world's ways, and
in most cases they seem totally opposite. However, God created
the world and those who live in it. He knows how it should
operate and what we need to do in order to have permanent
success and lasting results. The world always has a "fix it quick"
or "get rich quick" scheme that at best will only produce temporary and shaky results. However, this is not the way we, as
children of light, should operate.

Those who are part of the kingdom of God operate by faith.
Based on the Word of God, they call those things which are not
as though they were (Romans 4:17). They say, "Even though
this seems strange, if God said do it, then I will do it." They
know that God knows best. His way is perfect. His ways have
already been tried and passed the test. He's been there, done
it, and His ways always work.

We are on the potter's wheel being formed and fashioned into
that which God has ordained for us to be. The Holy Spirit
teaches us how to operate in the spiritual realm because from
our earthly birth we have lived in and operated in the physical
realm. Yes, God's ways seem strange to us in the beginning, and
they can be totally opposite from all we have learned in the
world. For example, God's Word teaches us that we must give

in order to prosper and receive; we are to love our enemies and bless them that use and hurt us; we are to always forgive, never holding a grudge. In contrast, the world would say just the opposite. It teaches hold on to what you have because if you give it away, then you will have less. Destroy your enemies so they cannot get you; get revenge on those who hurt you. We need to show the world that they are doing it wrong. God has a way that is perfect and leads to life, while the world's ways lead to death. God is teaching us His ways so that we can teach and show them to others.

There comes a time when you are going to have to do it God's way. No other way will work. So start doing things God's way now! For your obedience, you not only will be blessed above and beyond what you could ask or think, but you will soon become a blessing for others and that's what it's all about.

# COME INTO THE MARVELOUS LIGHT

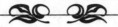

*I am come a light into the world, that whosoever believeth on me should not abide in darkness.*

—John 12:46

People who do not have Jesus as their personal Savior abide in darkness. People who may have Jesus as their personal Savior but do not know the Word of God abide in darkness. Notice that John 12:46 does not say that whosoever believeth on Jesus would not abide in darkness, but it says they *should not* abide in darkness. That tells me that they could abide in darkness if they don't have the Word to light the way for them.

The Word of God is a "lamp unto my feet, and a light unto my path" (Psalms 119:105). Without the Word of God, you will continue to operate by the world's system, which is ruled presently by the devil. He will purposely keep you in darkness because you belong to God. The devil does not want to see you live in victory, prosperity, peace or abundance. The enemy of your soul does not want you to learn about your inheritance as a child of God. He wants you to keep on serving him, even though you have confessed your faith in Christ.

Salvation is a process; it begins with confessing Jesus as your Savior and receiving eternal life. However, this process continues on from there, changing you and conforming you into the image of Christ as you grow spiritually.

Don't settle for just enough of Jesus to keep you out of Hell. He died so that you could have abundant life here on earth and become all He created you to be. God's abundant provisions are there for you, but you have to receive them. How can you receive what you don't know you have? You must desire to live in the light. In most cases, living in the light will mean being different because most people allow the darkness to suck them up. You should not abide in darkness. You have the light of God inside of you to give light to every dark place.

Get into a Bible-teaching church. Read God's Word. Partner with a ministry that is teaching the Word of God. Pray daily. Learn what you are entitled to as a child of God. Don't let the devil steal your inheritance and blessings by staying blind. You may be a babe in Christ now, but soon you will be a mature adult, knowing who you are in Christ and what God has promised you. Then you can start taking back what Satan has stolen from you all these years, and you will know how to walk in the light while in the midst of a dark world. Once you can see clearly, lead someone else out of darkness and into the marvelous light.

# DON'T BE A PHONY

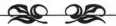

*Be thou an example of the believers, in word, in conversation, in charity, in spirit, in faith, in purity.*

—1 Timothy 4:12

*O*ne of the main reasons more people don't come to church is because of hypocrites. You know the type—they cut up all week long and then on Sunday morning, they are praising the Lord and shouting "Hallelujah" to everyone they meet. People who profess to be Christian are sometimes worse than those who profess to be sinners. Something is wrong with that picture. We who are true believers, who actually have Christ in us, should not be one way on Sunday and another way Monday through Saturday. Now, I am not saying that true Christians are perfect. I am saying that a true Christian, living by the Holy Sprit of God, should have some resemblance or characteristics of God in their life.

If you are saved, people should know it. They should not be shocked to find out you go to church. If they are, your life is sending out the wrong message and you should check yourself. The time for playing church is over. If we are going to walk in real victory and be blessed and multiply, we are going to have to be real and serious about Christ. We as a church have played church for far too long. God is going to separate the wheat from the tares, or the real Christians from the phonies.

You don't want to be a phony. You must be real with God and give your life to Christ. You must allow Him to change you so that your word, conversation, and character resemble Christ. There is no other way. God knows the truth. You cannot fool Him. It is time for a new beginning and a new way of life. Make the decision today to be a real Christian and not a phony.

# Forgiveness & Repentance

# DO IT GOD'S WAY

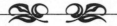

*Humble yourselves, therefore, under the mighty hand of God, that*
*He may exalt you in due time.*

—Peter 5:6

The word "humble" means to be meek or modest in behavior, attitude, or spirit; not arrogant or prideful. If we are to humble ourselves under God, then we are to honor God, obey His Word and submit to His ways. For example, when someone hurts us emotionally, we are not to seek revenge and try to hurt them back. We are to humble ourselves under God's mighty hand and allow Him to deal with the person who hurt us. In fact, we are to humble ourselves even further and pray for them. "But I say unto you, love your enemies, bless them that curse you, do good to them that hate you, and pray for them which despitefully use you, and persecute you" (Matthew 5:44). I know that isn't easy. Our flesh wants to retaliate and inflict the same pain to the person who hurt us. However, we must fight this urge and humble ourselves under God. It will become easier the more you do it. Notice I said "do it." It's one thing to know something and say it; it's another thing to know it and put it into practice. You will get some practice sooner or later.

God is a God of justice. He will bring justice for you. You must forgive as God commands and pray for them. In due time, God will exalt you.

The Bible says, "And let us not be weary in well doing: for in due season we shall reap, if we faint not" (Galatians 6:9). The challenge for us is to keep our faith in God. "Due season" means we will have to wait. It could be a day, a month, a year, or even years, but God will come through. Let this truth encourage you to do it God's way regarding whatever He is calling you to do. Maybe it's not about forgiveness, but about tithing, or your ministry or simply believing Him. God can only act when we commission Him to help us. Humility allows us to do that and then the blessings can begin to flow.

# YOU ARE NOT CONDEMNED

*There is therefore now no condemnation to them which are in Christ Jesus, who walk not after the flesh, but after the Spirit.*
—Romans 8:1

*If* you are feeling bad about some things you've done in the past—*Stop It!* You do not have to go around beating yourself up over your sins. The solution to your problem is simple. Do what 1 John 1:9 tell you to do—go to God and confess your sins. "If we confess our sins, He is faithful and just to forgive us our sins, and to cleanse us from all unrighteousness." God promises that He is faithful to forgive you the moment you ask Him. God not only forgives you for the sins you confess, He will also cleanse you from all unrighteousness, even the stuff you don't know about.

After God has forgiven you, you must then forgive yourself. I know that is often easier said than done. Sometimes the sinful thought, attitude or action has hurt you deeply or caused pain for someone else and you wish you could go back and have another chance. But you can't, so let it go. You can ask God to change the other person's heart and ask that person to forgive you. But even if they don't, you can still release it and move on. If your spirit is right, God will honor you.

From now on, when you sin, don't walk around feeling condemned. Instead, remember to act on what you know and not on how you feel. Feelings will change, but God's Word will never change. Immediately confess your sins to your Heavenly Father, get cleansed and just keep on going. If God says He forgives you, then you're forgiven whether you feel it or not. You must know you're forgiven simply because God said it and you trust His Word. Since God has forgiven you—go ahead and forgive yourself.

# IN WHOM IS YOUR CONFIDENCE

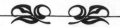

*It is better to trust in the Lord than to put confidence in princes.*

—Psalms 118:8

People will let you down. People will hurt, lie, use, make fun of, deceive and curse you. Even the people who love us will inevitably disappoint us. Why? Because we are imperfect beings who are incapable of knowing exactly what to do or say all the time. We do not know another person's heart, even if we think we do. So we, too, will inevitably disappoint someone, hopefully unintentionally, simply because we do not know what they are thinking or feeling, which could cause us to say or do something to upset them. It is good for us to remember that when someone unintentionally hurts us.

When we trust in man more than we trust in God, we are setting ourselves up for a huge letdown. That is why so many people are hurting today. They put their trust, hearts or lives in the hands of someone who is incapable of caring for them. We are not omniscient—having total knowledge. Only God is omniscient and knows everything. The Bible tells us that we know in part (1 Corinthians 13:9). Therefore, how can we be everything to everybody? It is impossible.

Put your trust in God, who knows everything about you and still loves you. Give God your heart. He keeps all His promises and will never forsake you. God will heal all the hurts from the past. He will bless you and give you things no man can—like peace, joy, strength and hope. You can totally put your confidence in the Lord.

# RECEIVE MERCY AND GRACE

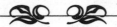

*For we have not an high priest who cannot be touched with the feeling of our infirmities; but was in all points tempted like as we are, yet without sin. Let us therefore come boldly unto the throne of grace, that we may obtain mercy, and find grace to help in time of need.*

—Hebrews 4:15, 16

Jesus went through every temptation that you have and will go through. I would venture to say He probably went through more than you because you haven't gone through every imaginable temptation in the world. Jesus went through them all! He had to in order to help you and me when we are tempted. Since He suffered every temptation, yet did not sin, He can help us to do the same.

Unlike the Lord Jesus, we do sometimes fall into sin when we are tempted. That is why Hebrews 4:16 says, "Let us therefore come boldly unto the throne of grace, that we may obtain mercy, and find grace to help in time of need." Whew, that is wonderful! God wants to pour out His never-ending mercy upon us when we are tempted and when we sin. We need to run to Him, not from Him. He said to come boldly, not timidly or pathetically, but with head held high and with the authority given to us by the blood of Jesus.

Thank God today for His mercy and grace. You receive new mercy every day. Don't waste it. Thank God for His love that adopted you into His family. Stop feeling bad about things you've done. It's in the past. Give it to God by repenting and ask for forgiveness. Let it go and receive the Father's mercy and grace. You are His son or daughter. He's not going to turn you away—ever!

# FORGIVE YOURSELF

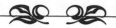

*If we confess our sins, He is faithful and just to forgive us our sins,
and to cleanse us from all unrighteousness.*

—1 John 1:9

*G*od's love is so superior to ours that we cannot begin to realize its fullness. God just wants to be good to us. But sometimes we have a hard time receiving God's love and goodness, because we don't feel that we deserve it. We think about all the wrong things we've done and said and we wonder, "Why would God want to bless me?" However, God doesn't love as we love. He loves unconditionally and completely. It is not based on anything that we do, but is based solely on His promise to love us. We could never do anything that would make God stop loving us.

Whenever we ask God to forgive us, He does. He doesn't think about it, or say, "You've done this too many times." He just keeps His word and He forgives us. The problem is we don't forgive ourselves. We keep putting God on our level. God doesn't judge sin like we do. Sin is sin. That is hard to understand, which is why God is God and we're not.

Forgive yourself. Let go of the past and press on to what lies ahead. If you have sincerely repented, God forgave you instantly and now you must go on. People who grasp this spiritual truth can have joy and peace even when they don't do everything just right. Get a revelation—until Jesus returns, we will never do everything right or be perfect. So get over it and just keep on pushing forward with God! We will change and get better, but we will always be on the potter's wheel during this life. And if you are going to enjoy the journey of life, you must learn to have joy every day, even when you mess up.

# GOD WILL NEVER DISAPPOINT YOU

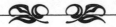

*God is faithful, by whom ye were called unto the fellowship of His
Son, Jesus Christ our Lord.*

—1 Corinthians 1:9

Too often we seek help from people who are inadequate to
supply our needs. Therefore, we often get hurt and let down.
People are not equipped to be our everything. They do not
know what we are feeling all the time, what we are thinking,
or what we are going through. Because of their limited knowledge, it is impossible for another person to meet all of our
needs. It really is not their fault when they say or do the wrong
thing at the wrong time because they do not know what is
going on inside us. But God knows. He knows everything
about us all the time. He knows just what we need when we
need it. He is faithful to provide our needs when we ask. He
withholds no good thing from us (Psalms 84:11).

God always has your best interests at heart. He will never
do anything to hurt you. Go to Him when you are in need. He
promises that he will supply all your needs according to His
riches in glory (Philippians 4:19). That scripture applies to
more than just your financial needs. All means just that—*all.*
By seeking His supply, you will free a lot of people who have
been trying to meet your needs, but in reality, cannot. Lose
them today in the name of Jesus, and receive from the Lord,
who knows everything, including what you need even before
you ask.

# YOU CAN RUN BUT YOU CAN'T HIDE

*Can any hide himself in secret places that I shall not see him?*
*Saith the Lord. Do not I fill heaven and earth? Saith the Lord.*
—Jeremiah 23:24

You can't hide from God. He is everywhere. There are a lot of Christians who are perpetrating, being one way in church on Sunday and something totally different Monday through Saturday. But God sees it all. He even knows your thoughts: "The Lord knoweth the thoughts of man, that they are vanity" (Psalms 94:11).

Listen, if you can't be real with anybody else, be real with God. He is the only one in a position to judge you because He knows your heart. He is the only one who can forgive your sins. He is the only one who loves you completely and unconditionally just the way you are. So quit trying to hide from the Lord. You can't! You may be doing an excellent job of hiding from people, but what can people do for you? You need to be concerned about the One who sees what you are doing all the time and has your life in His hands—Almighty God.

Today is a day of freedom for you if you choose. You can be free to be who you really are! If you've been putting on a facade to please people, you can stop today! God made you to be just who you are, no one else. You are uniquely made. You are fearfully and wonderfully made. Be yourself!

By the way, if you are hiding from God, or should I say, if you think you are hiding from God, you're not, so get real with Him. Pour yourself out and spend some quality time with Him.

If you are covering up a sin in your life, God knows, so repent and put that sin under the blood of Jesus. God will deliver you and forgive you—just ask. It just feels good to the soul to come clean and have a fresh start. The bottom line is, you cannot run forever, and you never could hide, so why try?

# WHAT ARE YOU ASHAMED OF?

*Fear not; for thou shalt not be ashamed: neither be thou confounded; for thou shalt not be put to shame: for thou shalt forget the shame of thy youth, and shalt not remember the reproach of thy widowhood any more.*

—Isaiah 54:4

We have all done some things in our lives that we are not proud of. That is a part of growing up. However, for some people the things that happened in the past still haunt them in the present. They feel ashamed and unworthy because of past events that have left them scarred and damaged. God has promised to repair us and restore unto us what was taken from us. He even tells us that we will not even remember those events—we will forget all about them.

God has redeemed us from our past. We no longer have to live in bondage to it. We can let it all go and press on with our lives. We have a glorious future in Christ. God not only forgives us of our sins, He forgets them (Isaiah 43:25). When we grasp this truth we can forgive ourselves and forget, too.

Hold your head up high, child of God. The blood of Jesus redeems you. Your sins are forgiven and you have nothing to be ashamed of. You are royalty because your Father is the king of kings. You have a wonderful future ahead of you, so go for it. God is on your side. You can do all that He has called you to do. Bury the shame with the old you, in the grave. Once you were born again, you became a new creature in Christ. Old things have passed away, so what is there to be ashamed of? You are not who or what you used to be. You are a child of God and that is something to be very proud of.

# DOUBLE FOR THE TROUBLE

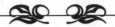

*For your shame ye shall have double; and for confusion they shall rejoice in their portion: therefore in their land they shall possess the double: everlasting joy shall be unto them.*

—Isaiah 61:7

*O*ne of the reasons we are to forgive those who hurt us is because they do not have the ability to repay us. Even if they wanted to, they could not undo the hurt and pain they have caused. God has said we are to forgive them and He will handle it. God can repay us; and not only will He repay us, He will repay us double.

If something has been stolen from you, start to believe God for a double recompense. He has made double restoration available, but you have not been asking or believing for it. Here is the key that you must use—leave the situation alone. If you are trying to get back what was taken from you, God will not be able to give you a double portion. The same holds true if you try to get your own revenge from someone who hurt or stole from you. You will only end up hurting yourself, and God will not be able to bless you. It is just not worth it. You cannot bless yourself more than God can.

If you will heed God's Word and obey His way, you have a win-win situation. You will be doubly blessed, the devil will be defeated and God will get the glory. You win, God wins and the devil loses. You actually come out better than you would have if nothing were ever taken from you. You receive double what you had before. Hallelujah! From now on I'll bet you will look at it differently when you are wronged or despitefully used. You have been set up for a double blessing from God!

# IT'S TIME TO FORGIVE AND MOVE ON

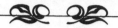

*Cease from anger, and forsake wrath: fret not thyself in any wise to do evil. For evildoers shall be cut off: but those that wait upon the Lord, they shall inherit the earth.*

—Psalms 37:8-9

If you are angry or holding a grudge against someone who has wronged you, forgive them right now. It is imperative you do, otherwise, the Bible says that God cannot forgive you. Let's look at Mark 11:25-26. "And when ye stand praying, forgive, if ye have ought against any, that your Father also, which is in Heaven may forgive you your trespasses. But if ye do not forgive, neither will your Father which is in Heaven forgive your trespasses."

Do not block your blessings because of something someone has done to you. It's over and done with so you might as well get on with life. Holding on to a grudge is not going to make what happened go away and it certainly is not going to help you get where you need to go. God will take care of the person who has hurt you if you give the person over to Him and let them go. Psalms 37:8-9 tells us that the evildoers will be cut off and that we are to cease from being angry and fretful.

From my own personal experience, I know this is not an easy thing to do. Nothing was harder for me than to forgive the man who shot and killed my son. I had to turn him over to the Lord and ask God to save him. I did it in obedience first to God and then God began to actually heal my heart so that I wanted to forgive the young man and see his life change for the better.

Allow God to heal your wounds and broken heart. Then He can forgive you of your sins so that He can bless you. Wait on God to make things right and you, too, will inherit the blessings of God on the earth.

# JUSTICE WILL BE SERVED

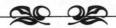

*For the Lord loveth judgment, and forsaketh not His saints; they are preserved for ever: but the seed of the wicked shall be cut off.*
—Psalms 37:28

God is a God of justice. He loves justice, and He will not forget you. If you desire to be vindicated, God will do it. He will bring justice in your situation. He promised you that he has not forsaken you.

I stood on this truth from Psalms 37:28 with regard to my son's murder. For nine years, no one was charged with his murder. It looked as though we would never get justice; too much time had gone by and there was no hard evidence. However, God worked through one diligent detective who did not give up and after nine years was able to get a confession and guilty plea from the man who shot and killed my son. He is now serving twenty years. I thank God every day for Detective Sullivan and all those in the Rock Island police department who did not give up the fight.

I know God loves justice, and I knew He would bring justice for my son Brian. He did not forsake us. I forgave as God instructed me to and I believed God would do what He said He would do. I did not sit around waiting by the phone every day for the police to call and tell me they were taking the case to trial. I simply believed that God would handle it. That gave me the peace I needed to go on and live my life in the interim.

Trust that God will bring justice in your circumstances. Nothing gets past God. He wants you to have peace and joy. You cannot lose because you have the greatest legal team ever created—the Father, the Son and the Holy Ghost!

# KILL THEM WITH KINDNESS

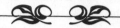

*Dearly beloved, avenge not yourselves, but rather give place unto wrath: for it is written, vengeance is mine; I will repay, saith the Lord. Therefore if thine enemy hunger, feed him; if he thirst, give him drink: for in so doing thou shalt heap coals of fire on his head.*
— Romans 12:19

If you try to get revenge for yourself, you will more than likely make a fool of yourself, cause more problems than you will solve and lay a sin to your account. Think about that.

Remember that you yourself have wronged and hurt other people. You may not have been aware that you even caused them pain. They may have been mad at you for a long time and you did not even know it. If so, which of you were suffering? Certainly not you since you were unaware there was a problem. The person who suffered was the one who held a grudge and unforgiveness in their heart.

There is a universal law call sowing and reaping. You reap what you sow. Let the anger go. It will only destroy you. If the person who hurt you is in need and you can help, the Bible says do it. That does not mean you have to get back into a relationship with them, but you can lend them a helping hand or just be nice to them. It will be the best revenge you could have anyway. You will heap coals of fire on their heads (Proverbs 25:21-22). As the old saying goes, "kill 'em with kindness." The ironic thing is, as you grow spiritually in Christ, you won't even want to get any kind of revenge. You will be glad to be a blessing because you are becoming more like Christ. And that is exactly who they will see — Christ in you.

Vengeance belongs to the Lord. Because God knows all the facts, He can be completely fair to both parties. You do not have all the facts, so you cannot judge fairly. God did not make any of us to be judge and jury of others. We can only be judge and jury of ourselves. That alone does not allow much time to worry about getting back at somebody else.

# SIN SHOULD MAKE YOU MAD

*Be angry, and sin not: let not the sun go down upon your wrath: neither give place to the devil.*

—Ephesians 4:26-27

It is okay to get angry sometimes. We often think that Christians are not supposed to have negative emotions at all. We think we are supposed to walk around in some euphoric state believing that everything is all right in the world and God will take care of whatever is wrong. Well, sometimes, things are not right and we need to get angry and say something. God will take care of it when we address it and pray.

Ephesians 4:26 does not say don't get angry. It says, "be angry and sin not." We can experience anger, but we are not to let that anger cause us to sin. When we see injustices in the world and in our personal lives, we should get angry. If we passively sit back and take it, we are allowing Satan's kingdom to run rampant. However, we should not take revenge or commit some other sin in order to fix it. We can direct our anger in positive ways to create change and to let the world know how we feel.

In your own personal life, you do not have to allow people to walk all over you. You can speak up in love, not cursing or screaming, and let the people know how you feel. Then forgive them, "not letting the sun go down upon your wrath." The key is balance. You can feel anger, sorrow and pain; but you, who are called by God, are to use your emotions as instruments of discernment and not instruments of destruction.

Let's stop passively sitting around waiting for "somebody" to do something about all the evil going on in the world. Be the "somebody" that does something about it. That's using anger in a positive way, which gives glory to God.

# SHAKE IT OFF

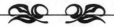

*And whosoever will not receive you, when you go out of that city, shake off the very dust from your feet for a testimony against them.*
—Luke 9:5

If you have ever suffered rejection and ridicule, then you know the emotional pain and hurt it causes. However, if you are a born-again child of God, they are not just rejecting you, they are rejecting Christ, who lives in you. Remember what Jesus said to Saul on the Damascus road, "Saul, Saul, why persecutest thou me?" (Acts 9:4b). Saul was not physically persecuting Jesus, but he was persecuting believers in Jesus. Jesus considered Saul to be persecuting Him when he persecuted one of His disciples.

It is the same with you. Jesus takes it personally when someone persecutes you today. Spiritually speaking, they are actually persecuting the Lord when they reject, hurt, use, or ridicule you. The appropriate response as a child of God is not to get mad or angry but to shake it off, bless them and keep on stepping.

I know that is not an easy thing to do. So the first thing you must do is give it to God in prayer. Turn the person over and realize they are not the enemy—Satan is. Pray for them to change and submit their lives to Christ. Continue to be nice to them and treat them well—even when you do not want to. God will honor you, because you are honoring Him. He knows that you are killing your flesh and walking in the Spirit because you love Him and want to obey His commandments. He also knows how difficult that can be sometimes. So pray for strength and peace for yourself, as well. You will feel much better because you shook it off instead of going off. And when that person changes because of your prayers and good attitude toward them, you will have a great testimony of God's faithfulness to keep His word.

# AVENGE NOT YOURSELF

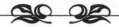

*Forgive, and ye shall be forgiven.*

—Luke 6:37

Have you ever noticed when someone hurts you, you want them to suffer the same hurt or worse? And you definitely do not want them to think they got one over on you. So you lie awake at night thinking of how you can get them or what you can do to hurt them and get revenge. In your spirit, you know this is not right. You have read the verse that says, "Dearly beloved, avenge not yourselves, but rather give place unto wrath: for it is written, vengeance is mine; I will repay, saith the Lord" (Romans 12:19). Yet, taking revenge is a temptation that is hard to resist, especially when you have become consumed with getting even. That is why I am being so adamant about this. You will never have joy when your spirit is consumed with evil.

You need to remember that you have been the cause of someone else's pain at one time or another. At the very least, you have certainly sinned and hurt God. You want to be forgiven, don't you? So the best thing to do when that revenge temptation comes upon you is to remember your own short-comings. You must recognize that if God had not forgiven you, you would die and go to Hell and live in it on earth. Selah.

The reality is this—if you do not forgive the person who wronged you, God cannot forgive you. The only person you are really hurting is yourself. You will be blocking your own blessings and putting a wedge between you and God if you don't forgive. And in this day and age, we all need to be as close to God as we can possibly get and get all the blessings we can.

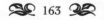 163

# BE MERCIFUL

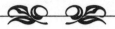

*Blessed are the merciful: for they shall obtain mercy.*
—Matthew 5:7

*O*ne of the greatest attributes of God is His endless and plentiful mercy. The Bible tells us that His mercy endures forever and that He gives us brand-new mercy every day. What reassurance this truth gives to all of us who need mercy on a constant basis. When we come to the realization that God is not mad with us and He is always pouring out His mercy upon us, we learn to receive God's ongoing mercy throughout the day. Therefore, we do not have to walk in condemnation. So, why is it that we who are filled with the Holy Spirit of God are so slow to be merciful to our brothers and sisters?

We need to remember that we do not deserve the mercy of God. If God does not withhold His mercy from us, then we should not withhold mercy from each other. We are instruments of love. We are children of God, who is love, mercy, peace and joy. We are so very blessed.

Compassion was one of the greatest attributes of Jesus while He lived on the earth. Wherever He went, people would throng Him and beg Him to heal them. He would heal them all! He always felt compassion for His people. If Jesus lives in us, then we, too, have the compassion Jesus has. We just need to let compassion and mercy reign instead of our flesh. God's Word says, "And be kind one to another, tenderhearted, forgiving one another, even as God, for Christ's sake hath forgiven you" (Ephesians 4:32). I would say that just about sums it up, wouldn't you?

# GOD HAS AN OFFER YOU CAN'T REFUSE

*As far as the east is from the west, so far hath He removed our transgressions from us.*

—Psalms 103:12

$\mathcal{I}$ am so glad that God is a forgiving God. No matter how many times I come to Him asking for forgiveness, sometimes for the same thing I received forgiveness for in the past, He forgives me. He is always faithful and just to forgive my sins (1 John 1:9). It does not matter to God what the sin is. If we repent in our hearts and ask Him to forgive us, He does. That, to me, is a true demonstration of God's unending love. And if that weren't more than we deserve, God not only forgives us, He completely throws the sin out. "As far as the east is from the west, so far hath He removed our transgressions from us." That my friend, is pretty far.

God wants to set you free. Free from guilt and condemnation and free from sin. Let it go and throw it out. Confess, repent and keep receiving God's forgiveness as many times as it takes. God has no limit on His forgiveness. He will just keep removing it as far as the east is from the west until you remove it, too.

If you have been afraid to go to God one more time for forgiveness, don't be. God is waiting on you to come to Him. Do not believe the lies of the devil that God will not forgive you again. You can go boldly to the throne of God because you are His child. Do not ever be afraid to run to your Father. He is not mean and cruel, nor is He sick and tired of you. When you really get to know Him, you will know just how wonderful He is. God only wants to bless you. He'd like to start today with wiping out your sins, as far as the east is from the west. If I were you, I would take that offer. You can't beat it anywhere.

# DIE TO LIVE

*For whosoever will save his life shall lose it: and whosoever will lose his life for my sake shall find it.*

—Matthew 16:25

$\mathcal{D}$o you want to have more victory in your life? Does it seem that you are not making progress or that your blessings are slow in coming? Well, do not worry, we have all been there. I received a revelation one day that helped to answer those very questions for me. I had specifically asked God to show me where I was missing it. Whenever our progress is slow or non-existent, it is not God's fault—it's ours. He revealed to me that I was still holding on to my old carnal life in certain areas. I wanted to have God's blessings without giving up the things He had clearly told me to let go of. I was simply being disobedient. God told me I could not receive His best if I did not give up my old life. I had to die.

We can sometimes deceive ourselves. I told myself that since I had given up most of my carnality that should count and be good enough. Nobody is perfect, I reasoned. Well, that wasn't good enough. I knew better and God expected me to do better. No more playing games and making excuses.

We have to get to the point as God matures us, that we give up our old lives completely. When we totally surrender our lives and allow God to take over, we gain the true life that God has planned for us. It is all or nothing. We cannot sit on the fence forever. God will tolerate that for a little while, but a time will come when we have to put both feet on God's side or you will halt your blessings.

If you truly want the good life that God has prepared for you, you are going to have to give up the old life. You will not be sorry, I guarantee you that. God has so much in store for you, you cannot even imagine. And think about this—what has your old life and way of doing things gotten you anyway? Hurt, depressed, frustrated, broke, unhappy, unhealthy, stressed out, etc. Give it all up. Get a peaceful, joyful, life of abundance with the Lord and really live!

# PAY WHAT YOU OWE

*Withhold not good from them to whom it is due, when it is in the power of thine hand to do it.*

—Proverbs 3:27

$\mathcal{G}$od is not pleased when a debt is owed and not repaid. If it is within a person's power to repay it and they refuse, it is a sin. If you are guilty of this, repent and repay what you owe. Do unto others as you would have them do unto you. Besides, you will block your blessings until you do what God has commanded. So do it today.

If you are the one who is owed a debt, do not get into strife and bitterness. God has also commanded that we pray for those who use us and forgive them. It will only hurt you to hold a grudge and be angry. If the person who owes the debt cannot pay, be merciful and show compassion. Situations happen that are out of our hands and control. Badgering the person is not going to help and it could actually hinder. Do what God tells you to do and then turn it over to Him. He will repay you all that is owed and then some. Be patient, prayerful and forgiving. You will come out ahead in the end.

Whatever you do, do not lose your peace and joy over the debt. If you owe it, pay it if you can; if you can't, sow a seed to allow God to bring you a harvest so you can pay. Then let the person know your situation and that you will repay the debt. Do not hide from them or avoid them. Most of all do not let the enemy use the situation to bring discord and strife. No debt is worth that.

# CAN YOU LOVE THE UNLOVELY?

*My tongue also shall talk of thy righteousness all the day long: for they are confounded, for they are brought unto shame, that seek my hurt.*

—Psalms 71:24

The world does not have a clue who they are messing with when they come against a child of God. In actuality, because Christ lives in you, they have come against Jesus. But I'll tell you how to really get them—stay in peace and talk about the goodness of God. They will be so confused, expecting you to be upset and rattled, but you're not. Just when they think they have got you for sure, just keep on having joy and speaking things out of the Word and praying for them. Before long, they will feel ashamed for having come against you at all.

When you keep your peace and walk in love, especially during a spiritual attack, you glorify God. Matthew 5:45 says, "That you may be the children of your Father, who is in Heaven." We should look like our Father. As children of the Most High God, we are different and our behavior should be different than the enemy's children. The Bible says, "But ye are a chosen generation, a royal priesthood, a holy nation, a peculiar people; that ye should shew forth the praises of Him who hath called you out of darkness into his marvelous light" (1 Peter 2:9).

You do not have time to be fighting with other people. You are chosen, of royal blood, holy and peculiar. You are of light, not darkness. Your name is written in the Lamb's book of life. Anyone who comes against you needs to see God in you. This is your opportunity to witness for the Lord. Do not blow it by acting out. Do not stoop down to the enemy's level. Do not play the enemy's game. It's an old trick, but it still works unfortunately, too many times.

Yes, you can love the unlovely. Be determined to show the love of God at all times and you will be so blessed, your cup will overflow.

# PRAY FOR THE EVIL-DOERS

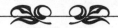

*Evil pursueth sinners: but to the righteous good shall be repaid.*
—Proverbs 13:21

*H*ave you noticed that some people who do evil seem to prosper and have good fortune, fame or happiness? Yet there are good people who are struggling, being treated unfairly and never seem to get ahead. It seems unfair and unjust. But remember this—things are not always what they seem. Some of the most miserable and unhappy people in the world have the most money, prestige, fame and fortune. My Pastor often says not to envy what other people have because you don't know what they had to do to get it or what they have to do to keep it.

Real joy does not come from wealth, riches or fame. Real joy comes from knowing Christ and who you are in Him. Real joy comes from knowing that no matter how unfair life is right now, there is a place made for you in Heaven where no unfairness exists. People who do evil and prosper will someday reap what they have sown because God is not mocked. But worse still, they may spend eternity separated from God if they never go beyond this physical world and its trappings. No amount of money, fame or fortune can give you real peace, joy or eternal life. You cannot buy your way into Heaven. So don't envy the evildoers—pray for them.

# UNITY IS A MUST IN THE CHURCH

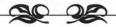

*Behold, how good and how pleasant it is for brethren to dwell together in unity.*

—Psalms 133:1

God is love and we that are brothers and sisters in Christ Jesus need to love each other unconditionally. Over the years we have been divided on denominational lines, color and race lines, and doctrinal lines. In some countries, they actually have wars over religious doctrines. If we who are believers in the Lord Jesus Christ cannot get along, something is terribly wrong.

God does not care if we call ourselves Catholic, Baptist, Methodist, Pentecostal, nondenominational or Believers, as long as we have made Jesus the Lord of our life. Some people have a religion, but do not have a relationship with Jesus. Christianity is about relationship, not religion.

Let's pray for unity in the Church. Satan has kept us bound with stupid issues long enough. I'm sure that no denomination is one hundred per cent right about everything. Trying to figure out which areas are erroneous is a waste of time and energy that would be better spent destroying the devil and his work in the earth. How long are we going to allow Satan to divide the Church? God wants us unified and praying. We can literally change the world if we come together and pray and walk in love.

Now is the time for a unified Church. God has given us the ministry of apostles, prophets, evangelists, pastors and teachers to grow us up and perfect us so that we become unified in one faith, in the fullness of Christ. Let's do that. It would truly be wonderful to operate the way Christ has designed his body, the church, to operate. Just like a physical body cannot do all it was created to do when a part of it is not functioning properly, neither can the Church. Let's forgive and heal the wounds that have caused division and mend the broken bones of the Church. Let's bring God pleasure by being a unified Body for Christ to use to heal the lands and do the work He has called us to do.

# HIS GRACE IS SUFFICIENT

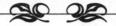

*For sin shall not have dominion over you, for ye are not under the law but under grace.*

—Romans 6:14

Thank God for the forgiveness of all our sins when we make Jesus our Lord and Savior. At the moment of salvation, we are freed from all sins, past, present and future. Therefore, we no longer have to be slaves to sin. It has no dominion over us. We may still slip and fall from time to time. We have a flesh that is used to sinning. But thank God for His grace. "Where sin abounded, grace did much more abound" (Romans 5:20). God's grace is bigger than any sin we could ever commit.

Before we became born-again, we lived in a constant sin state. It did not bother us to casually sin—gossip, lie, cheat, steal, fornicate, backbite, get drunk, etc. That was the norm because everybody did it. The big stuff did bother us, thank God, so we abhorred things like murder and rape. That is what we would have considered "sin." The devil could control us very easily and set us off at the drop of a hat. We were actually little puppets that the devil could manipulate and maneuver anyway, anytime he pleased. But now we know the Kingdom of God operates on a different level with commandments that allow us to receive the blessings of God and keep us from a whole lot of heartache.

God's unlimited grace is always available to you. His grace is able to cover any sin you may have done. The devil will try to convince you otherwise, but as we have said many times before, he is a liar. You are not under the law of sin and death

anymore. You are under grace. "Christ hath redeemed us from the curse of the law, being made a curse for us" (Galatians 3:13). Jesus took on all your sins. They have already been covered. Not so that you can sin all the more, but so that you can be free from the dominion of the devil. If you are free from him, then do not act like him or do what he tells you to do. Walk in the spirit, knowing who you are in Christ and be free.

# AUTOMATIC FORGIVENESS

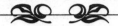

*And he kneeled down, and cried with a loud voice, Lord, lay not this sin to their charge. And when he had said this, he fell asleep.*

—Acts. 7:60

*A* great example of true forgiveness is seen in the Apostle Stephen. He was stoned and beaten to death by the Sanhedrin. His fellow Jewish brothers, even Saul, who later became the Apostle Paul, looked on. They could not stand the truth he spoke against them. To shut him up, they decided to stone him to death. But before he died, he cried out with a loud voice, that the Lord lay not this sin against them. Now that is forgiveness in the real sense of the word.

When the Spirit of God is dwelling in us, we have all the characteristics of God's personality dwelling in us as well. They are listed as the fruit of the Spirit in Galatians 5:22-23. Love is the first fruit listed and rightly so. If we have love for each other, the other fruit will be automatic. When you are walking in love, there is no way you can hold a grudge or seek revenge. Love will cast out any fear and love never fails. It is the cure for what is ailing you and is the key to joy and peace.

If you desire to have peace and joy in your life, you are going to have to keep love in your heart. Stephen had love for his brethren, otherwise he could not have asked God, in the midst of being murdered, to forgive them. Jesus did the same thing. He asked the Father to forgive those who were murdering him, saying they know not what they are doing (Luke 23:34). Jesus died for one reason—because He loved the world. When you love in spirit and in truth, you will be able to forgive. It will be automatic because of love.

# ARE YOU HURTING GOD'S FEELINGS?

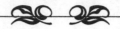

*And grieve not the Holy Spirit of God, by whom ye are sealed unto the day of redemption.*

—Ephesians 4:30

When you accepted Jesus into your life, your salvation was sealed by the Holy Spirit of God. You literally became one with God by His Spirit which dwells in you. He can never leave you, nor forsake you. Therefore, everywhere you go, God goes. Everything you say, God says, and everything that you do, God does because He is one with you.

When you do or say things that are outside of God's will and purpose, you grieve the Holy Spirit that is in you. God does not want to have any part of sin. God is Holy and Righteous and Good. When we sin, we go against the very nature of God, and that new nature in us, is not happy about it. The Holy Spirit will convict us and make us feel real uncomfortable. That is why you will feel bad after you have sinned. God is not pleased.

I believe it also grieves the Holy Spirit when we complain and are not thankful. Complaining says that we feel God is not treating us right or the way we feel we deserve. We need to be thankful for everything God has already done for us. We need to thank Him for life, shelter, food, clothing, a job, our family and everything else. Thank God in and for everything, every day. Wouldn't it hurt your feelings if your children never thanked you?

God is so good to us, that we cannot easily grieve Him. As we grow more and more in love with Him and begin to reverence and fear Him, our spirits grieve whenever we sin against

God. At least they should. When you really love someone, you never want to hurt them and if you do, you should feel bad about it. You want to apologize and make things right with the person again. It's the same with God. Apologize—repent—and get right with your Father when you have grieved Him. It is the only way you will have a joyful heart.

# TALK TO THE HAND

*But avoid foolish questions, and genealogies, and contentions, and strivings about the law; for they are unprofitable and vain.*

—Titus 3:9

Have you ever been in a heated debate regarding the Bible or your beliefs? I have. And let me tell you, it was a total waste of my time. In the end, I got frustrated, the person got upset and mad at me and nothing was resolved. Many times, Satan will try to get you into an argument about "religion" in order to confuse and shame you. People will try to disprove Scripture by asking a bunch of dumb questions. The Bible tells us to avoid even answering them. Why? Because, the person does not really want to know the truth—they just want to prove a point. Even if you prove your point, they will not be convinced. If the Word of God could not convince them, your word is not going to, either. If they really want to know the truth, God will reveal it to them in His Word. So now, I just tell them to read the Bible for themselves and ask God to show them what they are looking for. Then I pray for them. As for me, God's Word is final authority and it is a settled issue. I do not need to get into any kind of debate about it. I have nothing to prove.

Avoid useless conversation trying to defend God and His Word. God does not need defending. He has already proven Himself and His Word for over six thousand years and beyond! He is still here, His Word is still here and He will always be here. When people try to give you their opinion, ignore it and let them talk to the hand. You know how we do when we do not want to listen to what someone is saying. We just put up our hand as if to say, "I am not listening to you." You don't have to literally put up your hand and offend them, but you know what I mean. Just don't go there with them. Keep in mind that God Himself has said do not get into strife over foolish questions. It will not produce any good fruit and it just might push the person further away from God, which is what Satan wants.

Learn to hold your peace. Satan always tries to make us look foolish by trying to trip us up with some stupid conversation. Fight the feeling to go there. Stay calm and know that God is your God, and His Word is truth. No explanation needed.

# MONEY IS NOT THE PROBLEM—GREED IS

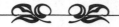

*For the love of money is the root of all evil, which, while some coveted after, they have erred from the faith, and pierced themselves through with many sorrows.*

—1 Timothy 6:10

*M*oney is not a bad thing. We all need money. God wants us to have money. After all, He made it. And it certainly was not made just for Satan's children. What is a problem is the love of money. In other words, lusting after it and having a spirit of greed to always get more of it.

One of the Ten Commandments is "Thou shall not covet…" (Exodus 20:17). We are not to covet money or material things. If we do, we begin to devise evil ways of obtaining those things. These worldly devices may seem to produce the desired results, but they only end in sorrows. Do not be fooled by the world's get-rich-quick schemes. They are roads that lead to destruction.

God has said that we are to, "seek ye first the kingdom of God, and his righteousness, and all these things shall be added unto you" (Matthew 6:33). Seek and crave after God and His way of doing things. He will give you the desires of your heart when you delight in Him (Psalms 37:4). If you follow God's way of prospering—giving—then you will have all that you need and more so you can be a blessing to someone else. God takes pleasure in the prosperity of His servant (Psalms 35:27). Do not get caught up in the love of money. Your heavenly Father has control of all the money in the universe. He will give you the power to get wealth and add no sorrow with it.

# YOU'RE ALL RIGHT WITH GOD

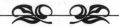

*For this is like the waters of Noah unto me: for as I have sworn that the waters of Noah should no more go over the earth: so have I sworn that I would not be wroth with thee, nor rebuke thee.*

—Isaiah 54:9

Right now, today, many people think God is mad at them. You might be one of those people. For whatever reason, they slipped and fell and think God has kicked them to the curb. That is a lie from the devil. Whatever you did, God knew about it before the beginning of the world. If there was ever a time He was going to be mad, it was while Jesus was hanging on a cross dying for whatever you did. If God was not mad then, He certainly is not mad some two thousand years later.

God is not like us. His ways are not our ways. His thoughts are not our thoughts. He is not mad at you. He loves you. He adores you. Yes, just the way you are. God made you. He knew how messed up you would be. We are all messed up. That is why we need Him. He has open arms waiting for you. Throw yourself at his feet and repent for whatever you did. He is faithful to forgive you. Once you have repented, pick yourself up, dust yourself off and rejoice. You have a fresh new lease on life. Your sins have been washed away by the blood of the Lamb.

Stop listening to the devil. Do not ever let the devil steal your joy with some two-bit lie. He is the one who is mad because you are God's child and he has been kicked to the curb. Remind him of that next time he tries to convince you that God is mad at you.

# YOU HAVE A FRIEND IN JESUS

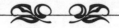

*A man that hath friends must shew himself friendly: and there is a friend who sticketh closer than a brother*

—Proverbs 18:24

*Y*ou've heard the saying, "A good friend is hard to find." That can definitely be true. However, you will never find a perfect friend because there are no perfect people. We saw that clearly illustrated in Jesus' life. His friends were His disciples. Yet, each of them had issues. Peter denied Him. Thomas doubted Him. Judas even betrayed Him. But He still called them friends.

The key to having good friends is to be one yourself. It goes back to sowing and reaping. If you sow friendship, you will reap friendship in return. A good friend listens, sincerely cares, gives of themselves, makes time for others and forgives. A good friend is not self-centered, possessive, selfish, mean, rude, backbiting or unforgiving. Again, to have one, you must be one.

It is the will of God that we be a friend and have friends. We are to work in harmony with other people. We are to share with one another and fellowship together. We cannot make it through life without each other. God has designed it that way on purpose. Seek good, godly friends. Learn to trust. It is a risk worth taking.

Remember you always have the ultimate friend in Jesus. He is the One who is perfect. When no one else is around to listen, He is right there. When no one understands what you are going through, He does. When you cannot tell anybody about it, you can talk to Him. He is a friend indeed. He will always be around and never let you down. You are never by yourself. Remember that when you are feeling friendless or lonely.

You have a friend in Jesus. Just call Him up.

# DON'T SKIP OVER THE IFs

*And the Lord shall make thee the head, and not the tail; and thou shalt be above only, and thou shalt not be beneath, if thou hearken unto the commandments of the Lord thy God, which I command thee this day to observe and to do them.*

—Deuteronomy 28:13

There are many people in the world trying to rise to the top. They are scratching and clawing their way up the corporate ladder. But that is not necessary. Promotion comes from God. If they changed their focus from the world and themselves and put it on Jesus, making Him Lord of their lives, they would receive a covenant promise to always be the head and be above. They would not have to play the world's games to get where they are trying to go. If it were meant for them to be there, God would put them there.

The key to walking in this awesome covenant is, "*If* thou hearken unto the commandments of the Lord thy God and observe to do them." We tend to skip the "ifs" in the Bible and want to just concentrate on the blessings. But God usually inserts "ifs" to designate our part in the covenant. There are always two parties to a covenant.

Don't skip over the "ifs." They are the key to receiving the blessings. God has a universal purpose in fulfilling his covenant with His people. He is not God just so He can give us everything we want and we can reap all the benefits while ignoring the greater purpose. He is interested in saving a lost and dying world from sin and death. He needs people who will be more interested in God's purpose than their own. When that happens people won't be so consumed with their own agendas and trying to get to the top so they will look good, but they will be more interested in God's agenda and making God look good. And one of the ways He may choose to do that is by putting you at the top so you can give Him the glory.

# Trials & Tribulation

# GOD'S GOT YOUR BACK

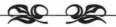

*Have not I commanded thee? Be strong and of a good courage; be not afraid, neither be thou dismayed: for the Lord thy God is with thee whithersoever thou goest.*

—Joshua 1:9

*D*o you know what it's like to feel that you are all alone? Has there ever been something going on in your life that caused you to become anxious and fearful? If we would all be honest, the answer is yes. However, these are precisely the times when God wants us to know that we need not be afraid, for He is always with us.

No matter what you are going through, God is right by your side. You may not feel that He is, but He is. Think back to other times in your life when you went through some rough storms. If you are reading this book right now, you obviously made it through. God is not with us just when things are good; He's with us even in trials. He will never leave you nor forsake you (Hebrews 13:5).

A very good friend of mine went through a sudden trial when her husband of fifteen years left her for another woman. She felt hurt, angry, betrayed and abandoned. But God was with her. Even though the storm did not go away, she was able to weather the storm because God had her back. She knew within herself that God had not abandoned her. He became her strength. He gave her courage and grace to endure. And through it all, she stood tall and made it through the storm.

Trust in God. He will see you through. Be guided by God's truth, not your circumstances. "The counsel of the Lord standeth for ever, the thoughts of His heart to all generations" (Psalms 33:11). Act on and believe in God's Word, not on what you feel at the moment. God never fails. Believe in Him and let worry and fear go.

# DO YOU BELIEVE?

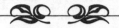

*Jesus said unto her, I am the resurrection and the life: he that be-lieveth in me, though he were dead, yet shall he live. And whoso-ever liveth and believeth in me shall never die. Believeth thou this?*
—John 11:25-26

esus had just lost His best friend Lazarus. He had been dead for four days. Lazarus's sister, Martha, had sent for Jesus to come, but He remained where He was for two more days. By the time Jesus arrived, Martha was not a happy camper. She told Jesus that if He had just hurried up and come, Lazarus would not have died. Martha knew that even now, if Jesus wanted to, He could raise her brother from the dead. Jesus wanted God to be glorified and wanted them to believe that nothing was too hard for God—not even raising someone from the dead. He also wanted them to know a fundamental truth regarding death—those who live and believe in Jesus shall never die because He already died for them.

We often feel like Martha when life-threatening events come into our lives. We pray for God to come, and He seems to wait too long, until our situation seems beyond hope. We want to know where God was when we first called. Now it seems too late and useless. However, it is never too late with God. His mission is to use your situation to bring glory to Himself, just as He did with Lazarus.

God has a plan that is greater than any plan we could come up with ourselves. He knows exactly what He is doing. We only know what is happening now. Even if our situation ends up in death, God can resurrect it. He is the resurrection and the life. No situation is too dead for Him to breathe life back into it. If He can resurrect a man who is four days dead, what makes you think He cannot resurrect your dead situation? If you believe in Jesus, nothing is impossible.

Pray for God to come and save your dying situation. But even if it dies, don't give up on God. Remember Lazarus, and know that as long as you live and believe in Jesus, you and your situation shall surely live.

# IT'S ALL GOOD

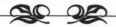

*And we know that all things work together for good to them that*
*love God, to them who are the called according to His purpose.*

—Romans 8:28

*O*h, what a wonderful scripture Romans 8:28 is. You cannot
help but be blessed and encouraged when it is read. This
promise from God lets you know that everything you go
through in life will work together for your good. It may not feel
good, look good, smell good, or taste good, but God will use it
for your good. He will use it to build character, compassion and
patience in you. He will use it to draw others to Himself.

Sometimes we find it hard to believe that the trials and tribulations we go through can be used for our good. However, God
will do just that. The very situation that you think is going to
harm you, may just be a blessing in disguise. In my own life,
God has brought blessings out of the things the devil meant for
evil. Now, I am not saying that God causes the trials we go
through. Nine times out of ten Satan is the cause of the trial.
The other time, it can usually be traced to our own disobedience. However, God will turn the very thing that the devil is
trying to use to kill, steal, and destroy and cause good to come
out of it so that we can grow spiritually.

Begin to look at your trials as blessings. Not only will that
drive the devil mad, but it will enable you to go through them
without stress, upset and anger. Ask God to show you the
lesson to be learned and expect to get some good out of it. It's
all working together for your good anyway, so you might as

well look for the good instead of dwelling on the bad. I tell you, if you will get that kind of attitude, God will bless you more than you could ever imagine, and Satan will think twice about throwing another trial your way anytime soon.

Let go and let God work the situation out for your good. Give it over to Jesus, stop worrying about it, and watch the salvation of the Lord in your life. No trial will ever be more than you can bear. You will get through it if you let God handle it. Remember, it's all good when you love God and are called according to His purpose.

# YOU ARE AN OVERCOMER

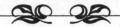

*These things I have spoken unto you, that in me ye might have peace. In the world ye shall have tribulation: but be of good cheer; I have overcome the world.*

—John 16:33

Tribulation and all it entails—problems, suffering, pain, tragedy and heartbreak—are guaranteed in this life. Jesus said, "In the world, you shall have tribulation." He did not say, "you might," or "if your behavior is good, you won't," or "if you get saved, you'll escape tribulation." He said, "you shall." So do not feel as if you are the only person going through a storm. People all over the world are going through the same things that you are. The devil does not come up with new tricks. He just recycles the same old ones over and over with different people.

However, God does not leave us helpless when tribulation comes. He lets us know that we don't even have to fret. We can be of good cheer. Why? Because the tribulations of this world have been overcome by the blood of Jesus! There is no problem, no suffering, no heartbreak, nor pain that God has not already paid the price for through the death of Jesus on the cross.

Have you received Jesus' offer of remission of sin for yourself? If you have not, do so right now. Say aloud "Lord Jesus, I know that I am a sinner. Forgive me of my sins. I receive your forgiveness of my sins and your salvation." It is just that simple. Now when tribulation comes knocking at your door, just smile and say, "Oh, yeah, I was told you would be coming by. However, you are not welcome and you won't be staying long. I plead the blood of Jesus. Because of His victory on the cross, I am an overcomer."

Scripture tells us that even though trouble will come, we have the answer in Christ. "And they overcame him by the blood of the Lamb, and by the word of their testimony; and they loved not their lives unto the death" (Revelation 12:11). It does not matter what is going on in your life, you are an overcomer. I did not say it, Jesus said it. You are an overcomer through Jesus Christ.

# THIS TOO SHALL PASS

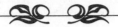

*For our light affliction, which is but for a moment, worketh for us a far more exceeding and eternal weight of glory; while we look not at the things which are seen, but at the things which are not seen: for the things which are seen are temporal; but the things which are not seen are eternal.*

—2 Corinthians 4:17-18

When we are going through severe storms in our lives, it seems as if we are not going to make it out alive. However, we do come out, and we are usually stronger and better for having gone through it. Trials literally give us much-needed character, strength and endurance. For as sure as you are born, there will be another storm if you keep on living.

Jesus wants us to learn that storms will come, but we do not have to give up. The things that we can see with our natural eyes are temporary. Jesus, whom we cannot see, is eternal. According to 2 Corinthians 4:17-18, we are not to look on the temporary things which we can see and feel, such as physical pain in our bodies, our bills, our jobs, our homes, our cars, other people, or even ourselves. We are to look at the things that we cannot see—Jesus, angels, peace, joy and faith—while we go through our momentary light affliction. Yes, it may seem like forever, but compared to eternity, it is only momentary. And compared to the suffering that Jesus endured on the cross, it is light.

If you are currently going through a trial, do not concentrate on the problem. Keep your eyes on the Lord. If you look at the storms that you can see and not God whom you cannot see, you will be just like Peter. In Matthew 14, Peter walked on the water at Jesus' command and then, taking his eyes off Jesus and looking at the storm, he began to sink. But glory to God, even when you lose focus and begin to sink, all you have to do is look up to Jesus and cry out like Peter, "Lord, save me!" (v. 30), and immediately Jesus will come.

You will get through the storms of life, and become a better person for having endured. Stay focused on God and not the storm, and remember that this too shall pass.

# TROUBLES DON'T LAST ALWAYS

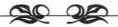

*This poor man cried, and the Lord heard him, and saved him out of all his troubles. The angel of the Lord encampeth round about them that fear Him, and delivereth them.*

—Psalms 34:6-7

God does hear your cry. He will save you from all your troubles. He will send His angel to camp around you and deliver you, if you fear (reverence) Him.

What an awesome promise from God! He lets us know through King David's testimony, that He hears our cries. The enemy will tell us that God does not hear us or is too busy to deal with us this time. He will even try to convince you that you are not worthy of God's attention, you are too bad, or because you have not prayed in so long that there is no way that God would hear you now. That is a lie. God hears everyone's cry, even the poor (Psalms 34:6). God is never too busy for any of us. He never slumbers nor sleeps (Psalms 121:4). He always has open arms, no matter what we have done.

What we tend to do when trouble comes, is handle it ourselves. We come up with our plan and we start to work. We put ourselves under stress and we worry. Then when too much time has gone by, we worry and fret some more. Finally, when all other hope is gone, we cry out to God. He was just waiting for us to turn to Him, so He could send His angel to deliver us from all our troubles. Why don't we save ourselves a lot of torment and anguish and go straight to God first. He is always there, even when we do not feel that He is.

Do not listen to the devil's lies. He is the father of lies. You can always go to God in prayer and get the help you need in your time of trouble. Only God knows how to fix it because He is the only One who knows everything there is to know about it.

God's promises are truth. He cannot lie (Numbers 23:19). If He says He will deliver you from all your troubles, He will (Psalms 34:17). Just believe and thank Him for your protecting angels who are encamped around you. Receive your deliverance now, for God has heard your cry.

# IT'S SETTLED

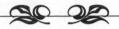

*But the God of all grace, who hath called us unto His eternal glory by Christ Jesus, after ye have suffered awhile, make you perfect, establish, strengthen, settle you.*

—1 Peter 5:10

Today's Scripture, 1 Peter 5:10, lets us know that suffering does come to an end. Peter said that it may last awhile, but it will make us perfect and establish us. It will also strengthen us and settle us. Let me quote from the Amplified Bible: "And after you have suffered a little while, the God of all grace (Who imparts all blessing and favor), Who has called you to His (own) eternal glory in Christ Jesus, will Himself complete and make you what you ought to be, establish and ground you securely, and strengthen, and settle you."

God does not cause the suffering, but He will get some good out of your suffering. God will use suffering and adversity to mold us into the image of Christ. Even Christ, who is the Son of God, had to suffer. Therefore, He knows our pain. The Bible tells us that He suffered and was tempted just as we are (Hebrews 4:15). Jesus knows what you are going through, and He wants to help you.

Sometimes, it is the suffering that helps us to grow. Just think about it—it was the bad times in your life that built character and wisdom. We grow in the hard places. We get to know God in the bad times. Let's face it, we cry out to God when we are suffering, not when things are going well. In my own life, I can truly say that I did not have the kind of relationship with

God that I have now until I suffered awhile. Even during some really rough trials, God managed to get some good worked into me by drawing me closer to Him. I learned that He is my rock and my refuge, my God in whom I trust. Those words became real for me and not just something that sounded good to my ears. I could not have made it through without God. He became, and still is today, my best friend and Father.

# HE IS OUR STRENGTH

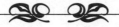

*Seek the Lord and His strength, seek His face continually.*
—1 Chronicles 16:11

When you begin to get tired and feel as though you just can't go on, do not reach for the medicine, reach for the Lord. God will strengthen you. God will give you whatever you need. All you have to do is ask Him and receive.

I think about Myrlie Evers, who endured the legal system for thirty years trying to bring the man who murdered her husband, civil rights leader Medgar Evers, to justice. Though the case was tried several times, the accused murderer, Byron De La Beckwith, was repeatedly released due to mistrials. It wasn't until February, 1994 when he was seventy-three years old that Beckwith was found guilty and sentenced to life in prison. Throughout this time, Myrlie never gave up. She had an inner strength that kept her going when others would have thrown in the towel.

The Apostle Paul said, "Therefore I take pleasure in infirmities, in reproaches, in necessities, in persecutions, in distresses for Christ's sake: for when I am weak, then am I strong" (2 Corinthians 12:10). Paul knew that Christ would be his strength when he got weak. He did not try to do everything in his own physical strength. It would have been impossible. It will be impossible for you, too.

It is no wonder we often get tired. It's a real "rat race" in the world. Pressures are coming against us on every side, and we are trying to stand on God's Word and be obedient in the midst of them. It makes me tired just to think about it. But God will give you the strength you need. He is the Great Stress Reliever.

Take quiet time throughout your day to close your eyes and receive strength. Meditate on God and His Word. It's the best daily vitamin you can take.

# IT'S NOT YOUR FIGHT

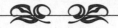

*And he said, Hearken ye, all Judah, and ye inhabitants of Jerusalem, and thou king Jehoshaphat, Thus saith the Lord unto you, Be not afraid nor dismayed by reason of this great multitude; for the battle is not yours, but God's.*

—2 Chronicles 20:15

When I read 2 Chronicles 20:15, I change the words to include my name. I say, "And God said, Hearken, Norma. Thus saith the Lord unto you: Be not afraid nor dismayed by reason of this great multitude; for the battle is not yours, Norma, but God's." You, too, can insert your name, because God is speaking directly to you in His Word. Make it personal. He is your God, just as He is the God of Israel.

Before we received Jesus as our Lord, we would fight our battles ourselves. Sometimes we won, but most times we lost and suffered greatly. Now that we have Jesus as the Lord of our lives, we no longer have to fight these battles ourselves. All our battles as children of God, are God's. He will fight them for us, but only when we let Him. If we try to fight them ourselves, even though He is able to help us, He will not. He will let us handle it our way, until we get tired of getting beat up and ask Him for help. Then He will step right in and take over, giving us another victory. We must then give Him all the glory because it was He who gained the victory for us and not we ourselves. That is all God wants—to bless us and get the glory and praise. How else will others see God work, but through us?

The battle plan is simple. It is spelled out for us in Ephesians

6:10-18. (1) Be strong in the Lord and in the power of His might; (2) put on the whole armor of God, that you may be able to stand against the enemy—the helmet of salvation, the breast-plate of righteousness, the belt of truth, the shoes of peace, the shield of faith and the sword of the Spirit which is the Word of God; (3) pray always with all prayer and supplication in the Spirit; and (4) having done all, Stand!

God wants the world to see Him and He wants to shine through you! What an honor, that God wants to use us to show Himself to the world! Give your battles to the Lord today. He is waiting to give you the victory. He has never, ever lost a battle. See you at the victory line!

# YOU HAVE THE VICTORY

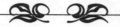

*For whatsoever is born of God overcometh the world: and this is the victory that overcometh the world, even our faith. Who is he that overcometh the world, but he that believeth that Jesus is the Son of God?*

—1 John 5:4-5

You may have heard this before, but I will say it again—You are a world overcomer. That's wonderful news. Whatever the world—or the enemy—throws your way, you can rest assured that you will overcome it.

When I am going through a trial, it helps me to meditate on 1 John 5:4-5. Because of this scripture I know I have already won the victory and I have already overcome the world. I must operate in faith and not look at my circumstances. Jesus said that because I believe in Him I have overcome the world. That settles it. I know that Jesus cannot lie, so His Word is true and it applies to me. And I can attest that every trial I have faced, I have overcome. Not once has God let me down.

You, too, can overcome the trials of this life. The sooner you start operating in faith, the sooner you will get the victory. You already have it in the spiritual realm, now receive it by faith in the natural realm. By putting faith in God in spite of the situation, you move the angelic forces to bring the answer. When you get the manifested victory, you will be able to give God all the glory, knowing it was He who brought you out. You will also build character—patience, endurance, self-control, etc. That is why you should "count it all joy when ye fall into divers temptations (various trials), knowing this, that the trying (testing) of your faith worketh patience. But let patience have her perfect work, that ye may be perfect and entire, lacking nothing" (James 1:2-4).

You will have trials (John 16:33). But God commands us to be of good cheer because we have overcome the world. So cheer up. God is on your side. And if God be for you, who can be against you? (Romans 8:31)

# DELIVERANCE IS ON THE WAY

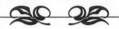

*Many are the afflictions of the righteous: but the Lord delivereth him out of them all.*

—Psalms 34:19

*I* have some very good news and some not so good news. Let me share the not so good news first. As a child of God, you will have many afflictions—it's guaranteed. Now the good news is that God has promised to deliver you out of all of them! If you are currently under attack or affliction, you probably are asking, "When?" Be patient my child, be patient. God will see you through and deliver you. But while you are going through, He will use the opportunity to refine you and develop your character. His goal is to conform you to the image of Christ: "For whom He did foreknow, He also did predestinate to be conformed to the image of His Son, that He might be the first-born among many brethren" (Romans 8:29) For some of us, that is going to take a little more work (smile).

People grow in the hard times not the good times. We need the trials in order to grow and develop the character of Christ. I believe when you come through an affliction, He will make sure you are protected for a while before another one comes. You will have good times, many of them. As you grow in Christ, there will come a time when you will be in the middle of what seems to be a rough time to others. Yet you will be sustained by the inner peace and joy developed through the hard times before. This is the place you want to get to—the place where nothing can steal your joy and peace.

Your deliverance is guaranteed, so do not fret. Hang in there. You have already won!

# STOP WORRYING

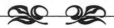

*Be anxious for nothing; but in every thing by prayer and supplication with thanksgiving let your requests be made known unto God. And the peace of God, which passeth all understanding, shall keep your hearts and minds through Christ Jesus.*

—Philippians 4:6-7

*M*y mother used to say, "Worrying only makes things worse." She was right, too. Having a problem is bad enough, then you get yourself all worked up worrying about what to do. Usually, there is nothing you could do, or you would have done it. But by worrying, you end up making the problem bigger.

God wants us to enjoy our lives and have life in abundance. We cannot do that if we are worrying all the time. There will always be something to worry about. However, God's will is that we cast our care on Him and enter into His rest and peace. It is not always an easy task. But as you work at it and God begins to show you His faithfulness, it will become easier to do each time worry tries to creep into your life.

We have to begin taking God's Word at face value and stepping out in faith. He cannot lie, but if we do not give Him a try, we will never know. What problems and trials are you worrying about today that God is waiting for you to cast over onto Him? Release them by faith into God's care. Stop worrying about it. Pray about it, ask God to handle it or to show you what to do, and then let it go. Enter into the rest of God and receive His peace. Be determined to have peace.

People might wonder how can you have peace and enjoy life when you are going through what seems to be an impossible situation, but you will know. Then you can tell them about the secret to your peace, Jesus.

# CALL ON THE LORD

*Give ear, O Lord, unto my prayer; and attend to the voice of my supplications. In the day of my trouble I will call upon thee: for thou wilt answer me.*

—Psalms 86:6-7

If you are in trouble today, I have some good news for you. If you will call upon the Lord, He will answer you and attend to your supplications. God will help you. There is no problem too big or too small—God can handle them all.

The Bible tells us that we have not because we ask not (James 4:2). God will answer, but we are not asking. We need to ask God to help us when we are in trouble, instead of wasting precious time trying to figure it out for ourselves. Go to the One who has a guaranteed solution, the Almighty, all-knowing God. He is the answer to every problem or trouble you have.

King David knew the source of his help. He always prayed and called on God. He was constantly under attack, and yet he never hesitated to call on God again and again. God will not get tired of helping you. He thrives on helping you. He wants to help you because that is what He has promised to do.

Don't suffer alone. Call on the Lord and talk to Him about it. He wants to hear all about it and be there for you. He will help you, so chill out. Everything is going to be all right. God is still in control. "Fear thou not; for I am with thee: Be not dismayed; for I am thy God: I will strengthen thee: yea, I will help thee; yea, I will uphold thee with the right hand of my righteousness" (Isaiah 41:10).

# THIS IS ONLY A TEST

*Beloved, think it not strange concerning the fiery trial which is to try you, as though some strange thing happened to you: but rejoice, inasmuch as ye are partakers of Christ's sufferings; that, when His glory shall be revealed, ye may be glad also with exceeding joy.*
—1 Peter 4:12-13

*I* know that the last thing you want to do when you are in the middle of a storm is rejoice, but if you could see the end result when the storm has passed, you would do just that. God does see the end result and that is why He tells us to rejoice when we are in the fiery trial. It is just a test. You are going to come out of it.

I always remind myself when I am in the middle of a fiery trial that it could be worse and it certainly isn't as bad as what Jesus had to go through. We forget the depth of Jesus' suffering for us. If He could go through what He went through, we certainly can go through our momentary affliction. Now don't get me wrong, I am not making light of your situation. I have gone through some seemingly unbearable trials myself. During the worst of the storms, the murder of my only child, I thought about Jesus, who was savagely and brutally beaten, stabbed, cursed, spit upon, had nails driven in His hands and feet, and suffered it all for people who hated Him and did not understand that He was God in the flesh. He willingly died when He did not have to, and went into the depths of Hell in order to snatch the keys of death from Satan and put him under our feet so that I, my son and anyone else who wants it, could have eternal and abundant life.

Life will be full of tests. Just remember it is only a test and not the end. No test that you will face is greater than the one Jesus endured for you. Since you have Him living on the inside of you, you will make it.

Let us rejoice and praise God that He is still on the throne and that whatever the devil means for evil, God will turn it to good. That's when God's glory will shine on you and everyone will see it!

# YOU ARE INVINCIBLE

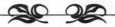

*When thou passest through the waters, I will be with thee; and through the rivers, they shall not overflow thee: when thou walkest through the fire, thou shalt not be burned; neither shall the flame kindle upon thee.*

—Isaiah 43:2

Wow! This scripture truly says it all. There isn't much I can add to it. I meditated on it, and it touched the very depths of my spirit. I was truly overjoyed. Of course, I made it a personal scripture written to me because it was, and you should do the same because it was written to you, too. Add your name and read it aloud like this: "(Your name), when you pass through the waters, I, the Almighty God, will be with you; and through the rivers, they shall not overflow or drown you. When you walk through the fire, you shall not be burned; neither shall the flame light upon you." Whew, Hallelujah! Do you see what I mean? That just stirs me up! You cannot help but rejoice when God makes a promise like that to you!

I don't care how bad things are in your life. They can be as awful as they can get. You have this promise from God that you will be all right. Nothing can bring you down. Nothing! You will not drown, nor get burned. God is with you every step of the way. You may not even realize it, but every day you are getting better. Maybe someone has told you that you are not going to make it. You just look them in the eye and tell them, "Oh, yes, I am going to make it. God has promised that He will see me through the water and the fire. I have the victory in

Jesus, my Lord." Let me tell you, God will get excited when you put that kind of faith in Him. He is looking to and fro in the earth for someone that He can show Himself strong in their behalf (2 Chronicles 16:9), and you will be the perfect candidate. Go ahead and be blessed!

Use what he meant for evil and let God turn it into something good. Allow God to demonstrate his blessings in your life, and give Him all the glory. That will show the devil who He is dealing with. He'll think twice about picking on you the next time he is looking for somebody to mess with.

If you are in a flood or in a fire, stand firm and know that God is with you and you will not drown or get burned. Shout hallelujah now because the victory is already won.

# TROUBLE IS GOOD

*Blessed are ye, when men shall revile you, and persecute you, and shall say all manner of evil against you falsely, for my sake. Rejoice, and be exceeding glad: for great is your reward in heaven: for so persecuted they the prophets which were before you.*

—Matthew 5:11-12

know the last thing you want to do is rejoice and be glad when trouble comes. But, look at this from a spiritual point of view. The only reason persecution, trial and trouble comes is because you start to grow in the things of God and prosper. Satan will do anything to try and discourage you and turn you around. That is why as soon as you make some progress, persecution seems to just show up with a big "hello" sign.

Do not get discouraged when some evil plot seems to come against you. You can rejoice because it confirms that you are a threat to the kingdom of darkness. If you were not, the devil would not even be concerned with you. There are too many other saints who are really tearing down his kingdom for him to bother with someone who is not causing any problems. So look at it this way, you must be doing something right. Otherwise, the devil would not bother you. He is just trying to intimidate you to go back to the way you were before when you were not giving him any grief. So do not give up! Do not give in! Keep on fighting the good fight of faith! Give the devil a fit.

When it gets real tough, remember who you have on your side…you've got God. "What shall we then say to these things? If God be for us, who can be against us?" (Romans 8:31)

# ARE YOU MAD AT GOD?

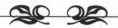

*Then said Martha unto Jesus, Lord, if thou hadst been here, my brother had not died.*

—John 11:21

re you mad at God? Have you blamed Him for allowing something to happen in your life? Sometimes when bad things happen, you get angry with God because you know that He has all power and He could have prevented this thing from happening to you. It is normal, I believe, for you to wonder why God allows bad things to happen in your life. However, you must remember that God loves you and would never intentionally hurt you.

As humans, we only see things in part. We do not see the whole picture like God. He knows that negative experiences can change us and bring out His godly character in us. He also knows that some of us will only seek God when we are at the very bottom and there is no place else to go. Sometimes God has to allow circumstances to break us in order to reach us.

God tells us that "in the world ye shall have tribulation" (John 16:33b). Tribulation does not come from God. It is because of sin that we must go through tribulation, and the devil is the one to blame. Even though tribulation is guaranteed in this life, God has given us hope. Right after He tells us that we will have tribulation, He goes on to say, "but be of good cheer; I have overcome the world" (John 16:33c).

No matter what is going on in your life, it is not bigger than God. God is your source of help. It just does not make sense to be mad at the only One who can help you. Do not play the devil's game. The devil is hoping you will blame God for something he has caused and that you will turn your back on God. His goal is to get you completely off course and out of the will of God. Instead, rise up and tell the devil, "You've really messed up now. You are going to be sorry you ever came against me. I'm going to be your worst nightmare. Every day, I am going to glorify God and tear down your kingdom."

Listen, beloved, God loves you so much that He gave up His only Son for you. He would never hurt you. Do not be mad at God. Turn to Him for comfort and help. He is waiting to pour mercy, grace and love out to you in abundance. Let God heal you and be whatever it is you need. He is not your enemy but your friend.

# STANDING IN THE STORM

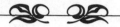

*We are troubled on every side, yet not distressed; we are perplexed, but not in despair; persecuted, but not forsaken; cast down, but not destroyed.*

—2 Corinthians 4:8-9

If you are not currently going through a storm, you have either just come out of one or are on your way into one, so take heed. Yes, storms are a part of life. There is no way around them. Without the storms of life, we would have little growth, compassion for others or love. Storms should help us to become better people and grow closer to God. However, they sometimes cause us to rebel and turn against God, hate others and stop growing. This should not be. You are not alone if you are going through a storm. The storm you are in, or coming into, is not going to destroy you.

Today's Scripture tells us that even though we are troubled on every side, we are not to be distressed about it. We are to trust in God to deliver us from the trouble and keep our peace. We are perplexed and do not always understand what is happening, but we are not to despair because we know the One who knows all things. We are not to lean to our own understanding but to acknowledge God, and He will direct our paths (Proverbs 3:5-6). We will come under personal attack and persecution, sometimes from those closest to us, but God will never leave us nor forsake us (Hebrews 13:5). And yes, sometimes we will fall and mess up, but God holds us in His right hand and we are not destroyed. Just pick yourself up, dust yourself off and keep on pushing forward.

When we know who we are in Christ and whom we have on our side, the storms of life don't have control over us. They become stepping stones to take us up higher, if we let them. God is there to see us through, so there is no need to be distressed and no need to despair because we always win in the end. The storms do end and the sun comes out and the flowers begin to bloom.

So stand fast, be unmovable, and you will come through the storm smelling like a rose.

# IT'S WORKING FOR THE GOOD

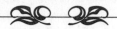

*And we know that all things work together for good to them that love God, to them who are the called according to His purpose.*

—Romans 8:28

When we are going through a very difficult time, it is hard for us to believe that it is working something out for our good. All we feel is pain and suffering which is not good by any stretch of our imagination. What we need to remember during those times is that God sees the big picture and we only see what is right in front of us. We may be feeling pain and suffering right now, but down the line we will see the good if we hold on and know that God has said that "all things work together for good to them that love God, to them who are the called according to His purpose."

I had a very close friend who fell in love with a wonderful, God-fearing man. He was everything she had hoped for. They became engaged and started to plan their wedding. Shortly thereafter, she began to discover that this man was far from what she had originally thought. After much prayer, the wedding was called off. Needless to say, she was heartbroken and hurt even though she knew that this man was not good for her. Today, she thanks God. She realizes that God allowed her to go through pain and suffering for a little while in order to keep her from making a big mistake. Now she can receive God's best.

You may be going through something painful today. You may not understand why it is happening to you. But believe me, if God has allowed you to go through it, it is working something out for your good. You may grow from it, you may change from it, or you may be thankful for it down the road. Just know that God will see you through it and, whether you see it or not, it truly is working for your good.

I know you would much rather skip the painful parts of your life, but if you are really honest, those experiences help you the most. So do as James said, "Count it all joy when ye fall into divers temptations (various trials), knowing this, that the trying (testing) of your faith worketh patience" (James 1:2-3). Be still and know that the Lord is God and He is working things out for your good.

# IT'S WORTH IT

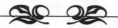

*For I reckon that the sufferings of this present time are not worthy to be compared with the glory which shall be revealed in us.*

—Romans 8:18

This life journey seems so hard sometimes. It seems that the minute we get through one storm, another one is on the way. We often wonder if we will ever get to a point in life where the suffering and storms stop. The answer is probably not. We can rest assured there will continue to be valleys following our mountaintops. However, remember that the storms of life prune away the things in our lives which are not of God. Just like in a real storm where the winds and rains blow off the dead leaves on the trees, the storms in our lives blow off the dead, carnal or ungodly things in us.

Once we have persevered through the storms and have been purified by the fire, we begin to change and become more like Jesus. This is the ultimate purpose of this life journey: to be conformed into the image of Christ. Well, that is not going to happen without major reshaping in our souls. We often say, "I want to be like Jesus," or "Mold me Lord, change me into a vessel you can use," but when God allows a storm to come in and do some reshaping, we rebel. These storms are necessary and beneficial if we really want to be like Jesus, because the truth of the matter is, we will not change unless we have to.

The sufferings we go through in this life are nothing compared to the suffering that Jesus went through when going to the cross. We do not even suffer as much as the early Christian Church did. They were put into lions' dens and eaten alive for their faith. We are not crucified, stoned, beheaded or burned alive because we called on the name of Jesus. Our sufferings are light in comparison to theirs, yet they still work the fruit of the Spirit in us, so we can glorify God.

When we think of how the storms have humbled us and worked in us patience, long-suffering, gentleness, meekness, kindness, self-control, joy, peace and love, we begin to be thankful for them. We can stop rebelling against them and face them head-on, knowing that they are working good in us and that God will once again bring us through.

Let the storms of life make you better, not bitter. For when the storm has passed, what you went through will fade in comparison to the glory that will be revealed in you. It will be well worth it in the end.

# REMOVE THE BURDEN AND DESTROY THE YOKE

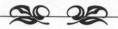

*And it shall come to pass in that day, that his burden shall be
taken away from off thy shoulder, and his yoke from off thy neck,
and the yoke shall be destroyed because of the anointing.*

—Isaiah 10:27

$\mathcal{I}$ used to be burdened with debt. It was not a lot of unnec-
essary debt, either. I only had one credit card, but a lot of
survival debt like the mortgage, car payment, furniture payment,
etc. Every month it seemed I was short even though I made a
very good income. I was tithing and giving offerings, but I still
was struggling to get through the month. One day, God revealed
to me that I could be debt-free. I had the power in me to cancel
and remove the debt. I realized that I could operate by faith, the
power of God that was in me, to pay the debt. According to
God's Word, I had laid up fruit in my heavenly account when I
gave into His kingdom (Philippians 4:17). That fruit was available to me anytime I needed it, just by making a withdrawal
from my account by faith in the name of Jesus. I had the power
to pay off the debt. I am now declaring that I am debt-free and
sowing seeds in Jesus' name.

If Jesus lives in you, then you, too, have the power to remove
any burden and destroy any yoke that is around your neck. God
wants you free. He wants you to show the world His power.

Unfortunately, too often we fail to use our God-given power.
Instead, we wait on God to do it without our input. But God
has given us the power! He is waiting on us to do the miracles.
He is waiting on us to heal the sick and deliver the captives

(Matthew 10:7-8). He is waiting on us to bless all the families of the earth (Genesis 12:3; 28:14). Jesus said, "Verily, verily, I say unto you, He that believeth on me, the works that I do shall he do also; and greater works than these shall he do; because I go unto my Father" (John 14:12). Jesus has done His part. He paid our sin penalty and has given us His power to tread on serpents and scorpions, and over all the power of the enemy (Luke 10:19). We are to do greater works than He did when He was on earth.

Use the power that is in you. If you have a burden on your shoulders, take authority over it, speak directly to it and demand that it be removed and be cast into the sea; and do not doubt in your heart, but believe that those things which you say shall come to pass. Then you shall have whatever you say (Mark 11:23). You have God's written promise on that. So what are you waiting for? Remove those burdens and destroy those yokes now. You have the anointing of Jesus the Christ, the Anointed One, in you. The anointing will destroy every yoke and remove every burden in your life.

# TO GOD BE THE GLORY

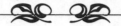

*Call upon me in the day of trouble: I will deliver thee, and thou shalt glorify me.*

—Psalms 50:15

This has been said before, but it is worth repeating. God wants to get the glory each time He blesses us, delivers us or keeps us, which, by the way, is daily. A day should not ever go by that you do not tell God "thank you." The fact that He kept you alive indicates that He is with you and He loves you. You do know that Satan would love nothing better than to destroy you. So praise God for giving you another day.

There are times, however, that we find ourselves in serious trouble. Our disobedient actions or Satan's attacks have backed us against a wall, and we need help. At these times, we should definitely call upon the Lord. It is not macho or cool to stay in the middle of a mess, when God is available 24-7 to help us. However, God will not lift a finger until you ask because He wants you to know that it was clearly God Almighty who delivered you. He promises to deliver us when we call on Him, and all He asks of us in return is that we give Him all the glory. Not because He is on some kind of ego trip, but so the world will know of His goodness, kindness and love. He wants people to hear some good reports so that they may come to know the living God who was able to deliver you.

I am always amazed at people who thank everybody for their deliverance but God. They thank the doctor, the psychologist, the teacher, the weather, the dog, the baby, a stranger, their lucky stars, but never say "thank you, Lord." It is perfectly all right to thank all those who contributed to your deliverance. It would be ungrateful not to thank them. But who do you think created the doctor and the medicine? Who led you to the teacher or psychologist? Who enabled you to have a baby and then formed it? Who sent the stranger just at the right time to help you? Who orchestrated it all in the first place? God!

Give God the glory. He is the one who deserves it. Anything good that happens to us is because of God. He will use people to bless us, but it is God who gives the blessing. I'll bet that if you start giving God the glory, He'll start blessing you more. When God knows that you will glorify Him, He will make sure to pour out His blessings upon you. As a matter of fact, you do not have to wait for some big blessing to come your way to start to glorify God. Glorify Him in your mind; glorify Him with your mouth and speak according to His Word; glorify Him in your body, which is the temple of God and treat it with holiness; and glorify Him on your job and in your home with Christ-like behavior. Glorify God in all things, and when you need Him, He will be right there.

# SATAN'S DAY IS COMING

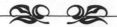

*And the devil that deceived them was cast into the lake of fire and brimstone, where the beast and the false prophet are, and shall be tormented day and night for ever and ever.*

—Revelation 20:10

Have you taken the time to read the book of Revelation? If you haven't, or if it has been a while, you should read it. It sums up the entire Church Age with more hope and prophecy than any other book in the Bible, in my opinion. I tell you, it excites me to know how the story is going to end.

It should encourage you to know that we win in the end. God is always in control. Whatever the devil does God uses for His good purpose. Satan has no authority to do anything without God's permission. God knows everything, beforehand. Therefore, you need not worry when trials come. God knows you can handle it. He knows that even though trials are difficult, they help us to grow and fulfill our purpose.

A lot of times, because of our sin and disobedience, God has to allow Satan to operate in our life. God will never go against His Word. If you put yourself into Satan's hands, don't go blaming God. God will deliver you because He has promised, but you have to take the responsibility for giving Satan the opportunity, if you have opened the door for him.

Okay, enough preaching. The good news is: you are on the winning team. Never give up hope that you will see victory in your circumstances. Read the end of the Book to help you to hold on. It's not over until God says it's over. God will never give up on you, so don't give up on God. Remind the devil of his impending doom when he comes around trying to intimidate you. I'll bet he gets out of your way then.

Rejoice, for it will not be long before we will all be watching the greatest fire show of all time.

# DISCIPLINE IS GOOD FOR YOU

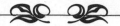

*If ye endure chastening, God dealeth with you as with sons; for what son is he whom the father chasteneth not?*

—Hebrews 12:7

If you are a parent, I am certain you have or will have to discipline your child. If you didn't, they would grow up to be wild, out-of-control adults—who show no restraint. We all know that disciplinary action is a good thing, when done fairly. We discipline our children so they will learn right from wrong and to protect them. Well, we are God's children, and we sometimes need disciplining, too. God is not going to just let us destroy our lives. He loves us and wants us to do well and have good success. However, just like a little child, we do not always know what is best for us or how to have that success.

Every trial you go through will work some good in your life. James said, "My brethren, count it all joy when ye fall into divers temptations (trials), knowing this, that the trying of your faith worketh patience" (James 1:2-3). You will surely develop some patience when you come through a trial. God can always work some good out of a seemingly adverse situation.

Every trial is not brought about solely by the devil. Yes, he is the culprit most of the time. However, God can also use these trials to grow you up in a particular area. You will survive if you put your trust in God and look to Him for help. God will not only teach you that He is your help, but that He is trustworthy and able to do anything. In the process, you will grow. You will learn some things about yourself that you did not know before. You will become better if you choose to. If not, you can become bitter. Do not let that happen. You will miss the blessing in the storm if you do.

God is your heavenly Father. He loves you much more than your earthly father ever could. He wants what is best for you. Sometimes, He will have to chasten you to get you on the right track. Don't rebel and fight the chastening. Allow it to do the work that needs to be done.

God will never put more on you than you can handle. Trust God and allow Him to prepare you to receive all He has planned for you.

# DON'T FEAR THE FURNACE

*If it be so, our God whom we serve, is able to deliver us from the burning fiery furnace, and He will deliver us out of thine hand, O king.*

—Daniel 3:17

*O*ne of the blessings that come from a close personal relationship with God is the experience that is gained from seeing Him work time and again in your life. Through this personal experience, you develop trust and confidence in God and His Word. So much so, that like the three Hebrew boys, you will be able to say, "My God whom I serve is able to deliver me from any fiery furnace the devil tries to throw me in!"

Daniel refused to compromise and worship the king's golden image. The penalty was the fiery furnace (Daniel 3:10-11). However, Daniel knew the Lord God. He was confident that God would honor his faithfulness and keep him from burning in the furnace. He was not afraid, and he knew that whether he lived or died, God's will would be done and God would be glorified. He told the king, "But if not, be it known unto thee, O king, that we will not serve thy gods, nor worship the golden image which thou hast set up" (v. 18).

We can have that same confidence in God when we are being faithful to keep His commandments. God is not going to go against His Word. He cannot lie. Things may get a little hot, and you may start to feel the heat. But God said, "When thou passest through the waters, I will be with thee; and through the rivers they shall not overflow thee: when thou walkest through the fire, thou shalt not be burned; neither shall the flame kindle upon thee" (Isaiah 43:2). Did you see that? You will not even smell like smoke! Glory to God!

Do not compromise. Trust God. Do not lean to your own understanding. You do not have the answers anyway, so there is no need to spend a lot of time trying to figure it out. Cast your cares over on God. Let Him be God in your life and work it out for you. He will if you ask Him and let Him. And in the meantime, trust and wait on the Lord.

You may have to go into the furnace, but God will be with you just as He was with Daniel and his friends. When you come through, you won't even smell like you have been through anything. Then people will marvel and say, "Blessed be the Lord because there is no other God that can deliver like this!"

# CAST OUT THE DARKNESS

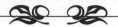

*When I sit in darkness, the Lord shall be a light unto me.*

—Micah 7:8

I know there are times when things seem so dark that you see no way out. You realize that you have absolutely no control and no direction. It is at those times that you must go deep within yourself, into your spirit, and find a glimmer of light in Jesus our Lord. Jesus is the light of the world (John 8:12). He is our light to show us the way to go.

The light is there, if you look for it. It may be small, but it is there. If you were in a dark room with no light at all, it would be as if you were blind. You couldn't see anything, even your hand in front of your face. However, if a lightning bug flew in, that small tiny light would be seen in the midst of all that darkness. Darkness can never overcome light. Light will always overtake the darkness. Well, when Jesus is your light, He will be greater than any darkness you are in. His light will cast out the darkness once you allow Him in. If you keep the door shut, you will stay in the darkness alone.

One easy way to find the light is to go to the Word. "Thy word is a lamp unto my feet, and a light unto my path" (Psalms 119:105). The very light that you need to show you how to get out of darkness is in the Book. You may have to take some time and study, but I guarantee, it's in there. If you seriously want to find a way out, then you will do whatever you have to do. However, if you want to find the right way out, go to the Word. The world may have some temporary quick-fix way, but it leads to destruction. Do not panic and run to the wrong light. Remember, there is a difference between light and fire. Light illuminates, fire burns.

Spend some time in prayer and, if need be, fast. Let Jesus be the light to show you how to eradicate all the darkness in your life. The more of Jesus you have, the brighter the light will shine—until there will be no room for darkness at all.

# TAKE THE ESCAPE ROUTE

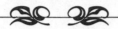

*The Lord knoweth how to deliver the godly out of temptations.*
—2 Peter 2:9

$\mathscr{E}$ach and every one of us must deal with temptation on a daily basis. The good news is that we do not have to give in to temptation because the Lord knows how to deliver us out of it. Even more importantly, Jesus has been tempted in every way known to man, yet He did not sin; so He knows how to deal with temptation and overcome it.

You do not have to struggle with temptation by yourself. God knows how to get you past it. Ask Him to help you in your time of temptation and take the escape route He gives you. 1 Corinthians 10:13 says, "There hath no temptation taken you but such as is common to man: but God is faithful, who will not suffer you to be tempted above that ye are able; but will with the temptation also make a way to escape, that ye may be able to bear it." Do you know what that means? When we succumb to the temptation and sin, it is because we have not taken our escape route. Therefore, we choose to sin (ouch). I know the truth hurts. However, the truth will set you free.

If you are honest, you usually know what to do in order to keep from sinning. It could be to keep your mouth closed, to tell the person "no", to avoid going into a certain place, etc. We fall when we do not escape before it is too late. It is never God's fault when we sin. And yes, you can help it.

The next time temptation comes knocking at your door, refuse to let it in. Pray and ask God to give you a way of escape. He will. Do not let temptation talk you out of taking it.

# AWAKE TO THE DAWN'S EARLY LIGHT

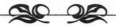

*For His anger endureth but a moment; in His favor is life: weeping may endure for a night, but joy cometh in the morning.*

—Psalms 30:5

*H*ave you noticed that your heartbreak and problems seem to be worse at night? While you are lying in bed and quiet, images of the problem consume your thoughts. If you do not consciously cut those thoughts off, they can send you into deep sorrow and depression. Yet once you doze off to sleep and awake in the morning, thoughts of the day's upcoming activities make you move on and the pain does not feel so great.

God does feel our pain, and the Holy Spirit of God comforts us. If we will think on God, or better yet, get out our Bible and read His Word, it is guaranteed to touch our inner being and bring healing. God's Word does not return void. It will do just what God purposes. Make a daily decision to spend time with God in prayer and reading the Word. Satan will do his best to keep you focused on the problem and create hopelessness. We must counterattack with the only weapon that sends him packing—the Word of God. If need be, speak the Word to his face out loud. The Word is your sword, and it will literally cut off the devil's head.

God has a good plan and purpose for your life. When we go through difficult situations, we must remember God is good and there is no failure in Him. We must believe this because our faith will start the spiritual forces working on our behalf to change the situation and get us back onto the road to victory. "For we walk by faith, not by sight" (2 Corinthians 5:7).

Psalms 30:5 really blessed me when I was going through tremendous heartbreak after my son's death. I knew that if I continued trusting God, my joy would be returned and I would be able to laugh again and enjoy life. No, it didn't happen overnight. But God consistently covered me with love and I stayed in the Word. I knew in my spirit that my son was with God and I had a purpose to fulfill that would bless others. This book is one of those plans He had for me. The one truth I held on to minute by minute was that God loved me unconditionally, just as I was.

The key is to stay in the Word and trust God. Believe what He says about you and believe His promises to you. You will get through the hard times and press toward the mark of God's high calling for you.

# ENDURE TO THE END

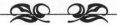

*Yea, and all that will live godly in Christ Jesus shall suffer persecution.*
—2 Timothy 3:12

If you were under the impression that once you became saved, life would be easy and full of good things every day, I'm sorry to burst your bubble. Yes, ultimately, life does become better as we learn not to focus on the things of this world. And each day is a blessing for the mere fact that we have life and a God who is with us to enable us to do His will throughout the day. But every day is not going to be a vision of bliss as you sit upon a cloud with angels playing harps around your head. In fact, it is quite the contrary. When you were saved, you became the enemy of the Enemy. Especially if he sees that you are going to be serious in your walk with God and make a difference. That is why you must put on the armor of God daily in order to stand against the wiles of the devil (Ephesians 6:11).

Even though the godly will suffer persecution, Jesus enables us to endure because He himself was persecuted. "For in that He Himself hath suffered being tempted, He is able to succour (help) them that are tempted" (Hebrews 2:18). Jesus even warned the disciples that it would not be easy because the world hated them. "If ye were of the world, the world would love his own: but because ye are not of the world, but I have chosen you out of the world, therefore the world hateth you. Remember the word that I said unto you, The servant is not greater than his lord. If they have persecuted me, they will also persecute you" (John 15:19-20).

Persecution must come. It is the small price we pay to be translated out of the kingdom of darkness and into the kingdom of light. The upside is that the rewards far outweigh the persecution, and in the end you will win. What you gain is so much more than the light, momentary affliction. In fact, you will not even remember the persecution you went through because the victory will be so sweet. The key is to endure to the end.

Your reward is great in this time and in heaven. God promises to be with you, so you need not fear. Just get dressed for battle and endure hardness, as a good soldier of Jesus Christ (2 Timothy 2:3). Remember, the battle is not yours, but God's. You have the upper hand because you know the outcome: you win!

# DON'T LET THE CREEP IN

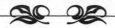

*Leave no room or foothold for the devil; give no opportunity to him.*

—Ephesians 4:27

We give the devil too much room before we try to cast him out. We need to stop him at his onset before he ever gets his foot in the door. The Word of God says leave *no* room or foothold for the devil. If you do not let him in, he cannot do any damage. Once he has gotten in, all hell will break loose.

The devil starts his attack in your mind. He will put his evil, sinful thoughts in your mind first, hoping you will mull them over awhile. That is the time to cast him out. Do not harbor those thoughts, not even for a minute. "Casting down imaginations, and every high thing that exalteth itself against the knowledge of God, and bringing into captivity every thought to the obedience of Christ" (2 Corinthians 10:5). You must take your thoughts captive. You have to control what is allowed into your mind.

Stop the devil early. If not, you will end up in sin. Yes, you can be forgiven, but isn't it better to just not go there? There are still consequences to pay for the sin and fruit to bear. We must learn that the consequences far outweigh the momentary pleasures of sin. We must get smart and stop letting the devil play us.

When those thoughts and images try to come into your mind, pray, praise and sing songs to the Lord. Whatever you have to do—just do it. Jesus will help you if you ask. Again, "There hath no temptation taken you but such as is common to man; but God is faithful, who will not suffer you to be tempted above

that ye are able, but will, with the temptation, also make a way
to escape, that ye may be able to bear it" (1 Corinthians 10:13).
One Scripture can be used for many situations. Seek the way
of escape. Stop the devil in his tracks at his onset. Give him no
opportunity this day to kill, steal and destroy.

# GOD'S WITH YOU

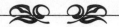

*Whither shall I go from thy Spirit? Or whither shall I flee from thy presence?*

—Psalms 139:7

We have all had times in our lives where we have felt alone and afraid. We would not be human if we did not from time to time. However, God sent His Word, reassuring us that He has our back. We are never alone and we need not fear because He is with us wherever we are.

There was a woman who was kidnapped from her home and taken to a remote location where her kidnapper had planned to rape and murder her. She was blindfolded and her hands bound as she sat in the backseat of the car, not knowing where she was headed. Her mind raced as she thought of what would happen to her in the next few minutes. Her heart was beating so hard and fast she wondered if her blouse was moving with each beat. She had never experienced this kind of fear before. She started to pray. "Oh God help me please," came up and out of her mouth. The kidnapper told her to be quiet. She continued to pray. "The blood of Jesus," over and over as she nervously sat in darkness, not knowing when the kidnapper would make his move. Suddenly, the car stopped. She heard the kidnapper open his door and exit. Several minutes went by. What was he doing, she wondered? Were there others coming? Again, a sudden wave of fear came upon her. But this time she said out loud, "No Satan, I will not fear you! I am a child of God! God is with me. I rebuke you and your seed in the name of Jesus! No weapon formed against me shall prosper!" When the kidnapper opened her door and pulled her out, she held her breath and waited. He cut the ropes from her wrists and got back in the car and drove away. She snatched off the blindfold in just enough time to see the car and the first part of the license plate as her assailant sped off, leaving her standing in the middle of a deserted, abandoned warehouse.

When we don't bow down to fear, God can do some miraculous things. He is always with us. We never walk alone.

# Daily Devotion & Worship

# IN ALL THINGS GIVE HIM PRAISE

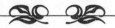

*I will bless the Lord at all times; His praise shall continually be in my mouth.*

—Psalms 34:1

You have heard it said many times before, "God is good all the time, and all the time God is good." That saying is absolutely true. Therefore, we must praise God continually. Yes, we should praise Him even when things are not going right and we do not feel like praising Him. In fact, that is the time we need to praise God the most.

There is an awesome account in the Bible where men who were imprisoned were miraculously freed when they began to sing praise songs to the Lord. "And when they had laid many stripes upon them, they cast them into the prison, charging the jailer to keep them safely, who, having received such a charge, thrust them into the inner prison, and made their feet fast in the stocks. And at midnight Paul and Silas prayed, and sang praises unto God, and the prisoners heard them. And suddenly there was a great earthquake, so that the foundations of the prison were shaken; and immediately all the doors were opened and everyone's bands were loosed" (Acts 16:23-26). That kind of praise pleases God. He loves it when you can rejoice and worship Him, even in the middle of a hurricane. Your true heart is revealed during storms. You will find out what you are really made of when at your worst moment you can still look up to Heaven and say, "Thank You, Lord."

Take a few minutes right now to think about how good God has been to you. Go all the way back to your childhood and work your way up to today. There is always more good in your life than bad. Praise God for how good He is today and watch unspeakable joy come into your life!

# THE REAL FOUNTAIN OF YOUTH

*My son, forget not my law, but let thine heart keep my command-*
*ments; for length of days and long life, and peace, shall they add*
*to thee.*

—Proverbs 3:1, 2

*W*e all want to have a long, healthy, happy life. For centuries, people have been trying to come up with fountain of youth serums to add longevity to life. More recently, people have gone vitamin and exercise crazy, trying to keep their bodies young and strong. God gives a very simple command if you want long life: "forget not my law, but let your heart keep my commandments." Not only does God say that obedience gives us long life, but it also produces peace.

Since God made us and knows everything about us, why don't we stop trying to have long life and peace on earth the world's way, and do it God's way. Instead of spending two hours a day working out—do not get me wrong, exercise is a good thing when done in a balanced way—why don't we also spend one hour in prayer and Bible study each day. This time will benefit both our physical body and our spirit. We will learn God's commandments and He will reveal His special plan for each of our lives. I cannot help but believe that when we are doing what God created us specifically to do—spending time with Him, and following His ways—we are guaranteed happiness and joy. This state of being and living can only bring peace, which in turn will provide us with a longer, more fulfilling life.

# I'M TOO BLESSED TO BE STRESSED

*The Lord will give strength unto His people; the Lord will bless His people with peace.*

—Psalms 29:11

*It* helps to read Scriptures like Psalms 29 when we get discouraged or tired. It lets us know that we have the Lord to give strength and send His peace. His peace is not based on the circumstances but based upon God who is bigger than any circumstance. What a blessing! If we keep our eyes on Jesus instead of the problems and cares of the world, we could actually live a stress-free, happy life. It is God's plan for you and me to walk in the spirit, casting our cares on Him and letting Him shower us with His strength and peace, day by day.

I petition you to try living a stress-free life today. In your prayer and devotion time, cast every problem and worry over to Jesus. Thank Him that He is already taking care of it for you and receive strength and peace. When the devil tries to remind you of your problems throughout the day, and he will, say to yourself, "I will not worry about that anymore. I gave it to Jesus, and He will handle it. Sorry, devil, I'm at peace and stress free." If you keep that attitude up, the devil will get stressed out himself and leave you alone.

# CHOOSE THE GOOD PART

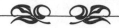

*But Martha was cumbered about much serving, and came to Him, and said, Lord, dost thou not care that my sister hath left me to serve alone? Bid her, therefore, that she helps me. And Jesus answered, and said unto her, Martha, Martha, thou art anxious and troubled about many things. But one thing is needful, and Mary hath chosen that good part, which shall not be taken away from her.*

—Luke 10:40-42

When I read this passage of Scripture, I realize that many of us are like Martha, trying to be superwoman, or superman. Martha typifies a workaholic who takes on too many tasks at the same time and cannot handle them all. She wants to take some time to pray or read her Bible, but the day has gotten away from her. Tiredly, she tells herself that she will do it tomorrow.

Does this description sound familiar? We can get so caught up in the things of this world that we forget the most important thing—God. The really bad thing about leaving God out is that we are actually omitting the one needful thing that will help us with all the other things. Spending time with God is choosing the good part of our day. He will give us the direction we need to prioritize and get things done with less stress and anxiety. He will also give us joy while we are going about our daily routine.

Mary had the right idea. She knew that the people could eat later or even skip a meal. She had a once-in-a-lifetime opportunity to sit at the feet of Jesus and hear Him preach. She was not going to miss that for anybody or anything. She knew what Jesus was saying was far more important than her sister's complaints. We need to be like Mary.

# PRAISE YOURSELF HAPPY

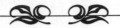

*Praise ye the Lord. O give thanks unto the Lord, for He is good; for His mercy endureth forever.*

—Psalms 106:1

God is good! He is truly wonderful and awesome. His goodness goes beyond anything we can imagine. He gives us new mercy every day to cover and bless us in spite of us. He loves us unconditionally and gives us favor. How can we refuse to love Him? He is truly deserving of our undying love. The best way we can bless Him and show Him how much we love Him is by giving Him praise. Praise turns Him on and makes Him happy. Praise will do a world of good for you, too. When you get caught up in praising God, you just feel good. You forget all about your problems and you are set free.

One of the best remedies for a downcast spirit, heartache or just plain old feeling bad is to offer up a sacrifice of praise. Your flesh may not want to, but you must press and do it anyway. There is no way that you can still feel bad after spending time praising God. God will meet you and His presence will come all over you. And believe me, when the presence of God is near, there is just no room for negative junk. He will cast all that out.

Find some time in your day to close off the world and praise the Lord. Sing a song to Him. Thank Him for all He has done for you. Worship Him for being the Creator of Heaven and Earth and everything in it. He wants to be praised. He truly deserves all our praise. It is because of God that we exist and have all that we have. It is because of Him we have eternal life in Heaven when this earthly life is over. It is because of Him we have hope for today and tomorrow. It is because of Him we can enjoy our lives even in the midst of trials. Thank Him and bless His holy name!

# WORSHIP THE LORD

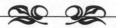

*Oh come, let us worship and bow down; let us kneel before the Lord our maker. For He is our God, and we are the people of His pasture, and the sheep of His hand.*

—Psalms 95:6-7

We are truly blessed people to be in God's family. We know the true living God as our Father. Jesus is our source. He is our everything. Let's give Him glory and worship Him.

It is just good to spend time worshipping God. Think about all the wonderful things He has done and tell Him, "I love you." Think about the petitions you have made before Him and even before you see them come to pass say, "Thank You." Bow down on your knees, lift up holy hands, and bless His holy name. Sing a love song to Him. Dance before Him. Praise Him. He is holy, and wonderful, and awesome. He is God!

One thing is certain, when you begin to praise the Lord as if you have lost your mind, you will get filled with so much joy that your problems and pain will go flying out the window. You cannot rejoice and be sorrowful at the same time. It will do your spirit so much good to start the day with a thankful and grateful attitude—just thinking about what God has done, what He is doing, and what He will do. It sure is a lot better than starting your day feeling bad and sorry for yourself.

You might as well enjoy this day while you have it. Give God the praise that He longs for and deserves. He truly is worthy; and to top it off, you will get a blessing, too. It will cheer you up and cause you to see the possibilities the day holds. The Bible tells us that "A merry heart doeth good like a medicine: but a broken spirit drieth the bones" (Proverbs 17:22). So get your praise on!

# TURN ON THE LIGHT

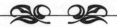

*Thy word is a lamp unto my feet, and a light unto my path.*
—Psalms 119:105

*G*od has given us the greatest tool for successful living. He has taken His character, personality and love and written it down for us as a success manual. When we get in trouble, and we will, the Word gives us the way of escape. When things get too dark for us to see, the Word becomes a lamp to show us the way out. When we have lost all hope, the Word becomes a light at the end of our tunnel.

There is nothing more exciting than spending time with God in His Word. It is not like reading an ordinary book or novel because it is God Himself in written form. I can come to a particular Scripture that really ministers to my spirit and read it over and over because it is just what I need at that time. It is as if God is speaking directly to me. There is so much wisdom in the Word that we could never exhaust it all.

One word from God can totally change your life! You do not have to know the entire Bible in order to receive deliverance. Some people know the Bible and can quote Scripture, but do not know God. He is the light—the Light of the world. With God in your heart, one word from Him will light up your path.

# MAKE YOURSELF HAPPY

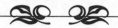

*A merry heart doeth good like a medicine; but a broken spirit drieth the bones.*

—Proverbs 17:22

The trials of life can really wear us down. Day after day we find ourselves in some sort of struggle against the devil, the world, or most often our own flesh. If we are not careful our spirits can easily be broken by constant setbacks, failures and disappointments. This is what the enemy wants. He wants us to become discouraged so that we will stop fighting and give up.

However, I tell you today that you cannot give up; you cannot quit. No matter what it takes, you must make yourself happy by looking to the Lord.

There is a time in all of our lives when we have to encourage and uplift ourselves. No one will be available to comfort us; no one will be around to listen to us; no one will be there to tell us everything is going to be all right. But we can talk to ourselves. That is what King David did when everyone had forsaken him and his own men wanted to kill him.

Read 1 Samuel 30:1-6 and see for yourself. You have to take responsibility for your own joy and happiness. If your joy and happiness are dependent on other people, you are destined for heartbreak. Make yourself merry and let your joy come from the Lord. He will never let you down.

You will find that having a merry heart on purpose, not depending on your circumstances, will cause you to feel better physically. It truly is like a medicine to your body. So make a decision today that no matter what you are going through, you will encourage yourself in the Lord and take the spiritual medicine that will do your body, soul and spirit good.

# FOLLOW FAITH

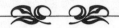

*That ye be not slothful, but followers of them who through faith and patience inherit the promises.*

—Hebrews 6:12

Walking by faith and not by sight is not easy. We are so accustomed to walking by sight that we constantly have to remind ourselves not to look at the circumstances around us, but to look at God's promises. The moment we take our eyes off of God's promises, we become slothful in our faith.

Like anything of real value in the world, walking by faith takes hard work. We must diligently keep our focus upon the things not seen instead of the things we see. If we keep the faith and do not let go of God's promises, the thing that is unseen soon becomes visible.

Do not be slothful in your faith today. Make a decision once and for all that you are going to believe God no matter how impossible it looks right now. You are not going to be led by what you see, but by what you know to be true—God's Word. You are going to press on in faith, knowing that God is going to come through. You are going to have patience because you know God is getting you ready to receive, and His provision will not be a minute late. Your promise from God is on the way. Stand fast, be unmovable, and inherit what Jesus died for you to have.

# GOD HEARS YOUR PRAYERS

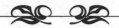

*For the eyes of the Lord are over the righteous, and His ears are open unto their prayers.*

—1 Peter 3:12

If you have been born again, you are considered righteous in God's eyes. You have traded in your sinful nature and put on Christ's righteousness. Therefore, you can boldly say, "I am the righteousness of God in Christ Jesus" (2 Corinthians 5:21). This truth is not based on your behavior, but rather the righteousness that is accounted to you because you have trusted in Jesus.

Because you are righteous, God does not look at your behavior. He only sees the blood of Jesus. You never have to wonder if God heard you or if your prayers got through. Whether you "feel" that they were heard or not is irrelevant. God has told you that they were heard. You must believe it by faith just as you believe you were saved by faith. Faith is not based on a feeling but on knowing what the Word of God says. When you know, then your feelings will have nothing to do with it.

God is always there. He always sees you and He always hears you. This you must know. So pray fervently and boldly because God does hear each and every prayer you pray. He knows what you will pray even before you pray it. So pray and believe you receive because you are the righteousness of God in Christ Jesus, and the prayers of the righteous "availeth much" (James 5:16).

# AFTERWORD

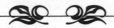

I am constantly amazed at the strategy and the greatness of God. His ways are beyond our thinking, beyond our finding out. What exactly do I mean? It is this. I had no intention of writing this book. I was quite content to read other inspirational materials. I had no aspiration to share my thoughts, my darkest days, my pinnacle moments with the public. You see, I am a very private person. But life sometimes places you in a situation where you have to get on bended knees, then rejoice and shout when the darkness has passed. It is in those moments that you know God is nearby, his holy words offering us strength.

*Joy Comes This Morning* is meant to be read often. It is a book that should be kept near your bed, in your office, wherever you rest so you may randomly pick it up and find a spiritual nugget. May it give you as much peace and comfort as it has given me.

*Norma DeShields Brown*